The Future

A Complete Breakdown of End-Time Events

Apostle Jimmy F. Artis Sr.

Creative Touch Publishing LLC.

Creative Touch Publishing

P.O. Box 7482
Warner Robins, GA 31095
ctpublishing14@gmail.com

Printed and bound in the United States of America

1. Spiritual. 2. Motivational. 3. Non-Fiction.

International Standard Book Number

978-0-578-70498-2

⌘ TABLE OF CONTENTS ⌘

Dedication..4

Acknowledgements..................................5

Foreword..6

Introduction...7

Chapter 1: Caught Up................................9

Chapter 2: Daniel's 70th Week.....................41

Chapter 3: The Seven Year Tribulation Period.......47

Chapter 4: The Second Coming of Christ.............75

Chapter 5: The Battle of Armageddon................87

Chapter 6: This Generation?.......................95

Chapter 7: The Millennial Reign of Christ...........111

Chapter 8: The Great White Throne Judgement.....119

Chapter 9: A New Heaven and Earth................127

Chapter 10: Wake Up Church......................135

⌘ DEDICATION ⌘

This book is dedicated to My Father's House Ministries Inc.:

A people who taught me how to be a spiritual father.

⌘ ACKNOWLEDGEMENTS ⌘

Writing this book has been a long-time inspiration, that was made possible by the support of many. None of this would have been possible without the covering of my spiritual father, Apostle John T. Graham, of Temple United Methodist Church (Wilmington, DE). You have supported my ministry and for that I am eternally grateful. Thank you for your wisdom, prayers, leadership, and friendship throughout the years.

To Carol, my daughters Debra and Shanese, and to my son Junior; thank you for your love and understanding over the years.

A very special thanks to one of my closest friends and co-laborers in ministry, Pastor Tiana Banks-Scott. You have encouraged me and worked alongside me, and I am grateful to you.

Finally, I would like to thank some special people who have shown me so much love, kindness, and support over the years. Elder Shannon Banks, Elder Sabrina Motto, Minister Chris Motto, Minister Jeffrey Bryant, and Mom Janice Banks.

⌘ FOREWORD ⌘

In this book, "The Future: A Complete Breakdown of End-Time Events," Apostle Jimmy Artis gives us a fresh look into the heart of eschatology. He leads us through the myths, mysteries, and misunderstandings of end-time events with a thorough breakdown of scripture. Line upon line and precept upon precept, here a little and there a little, Apostle Jimmy Artis stays true to the simplicity of the Word of God, yet takes us on a journey of scholarly work that is quite profound.

If his goal was to open the eyes of our understanding in this thesis, I will say, job well done.

Revealing the truth, while dismantling the lies surrounding eschatology, this book is a great resource for senior leaders, as well as the serious student. This is such a timely book for the age we are living in.

Job well done Apostle Jimmy Artis.

Apostle Daniel L Akins,
Presiding Prelate of More Sure Word Church and the
Voice of Many Waters Apostolic Alliance

⌘ INTRODUCTION ⌘

Tomorrow, the future; words that for so many, carry all the hope imaginable, but for others, all the despair. For some, tomorrow (the future) will bring wedding vows, or the long-awaited birth of a child. For others, it will be a notice of foreclosure on their home, or the tragic death of a loved. Life has a way of issuing detours; despite all the planning we do to secure the future of our dreams. The Body of Christ has a bright and certain future. Those of us who trust and believe in God's Word, not only hope in this life, but we look forward to the future as foretold in the Bible.

There is much controversy and debate in the Body of the Christ concerning the future events spoken of in the Word of God. For example, there are many who question, what is the rapture, and has it already happened? Others ask, is there even going to be one? Regarding the Antichrist, many ask, who is he, and what does he have to do with the Tribulation Period? The church has referenced the return of Christ for centuries, leaving many to question if it is just a scare tactic the church uses. The content of this book will answer these questions and many more.

Eschatology is the study of end time events. It is a breakdown of the things which are to occur in this world as Christ prepares for His return. It also includes the events which are to occur following His return. The Word of God gives us numerous clues concerning these events. These clues are shared throughout several books of the Bible, including the book of Revelation. As a prophet of God, I was charged over twenty-five years ago to prepare a people for His return. I endeavor to give the Body of Christ the knowledge necessary to be just that. . . prepared for the return of Jesus the Christ.

⌘ CHAPTER ONE ⌘

Caught Up

In this chapter, we will look at varying views regarding the *rapture* of the church. Although the word *"rapture"* is not found in the Bible, the event itself is. This book will address it in detail. First, we must ask, where does the word *rapture* come from? The word *rapture* is derived from the Latin word *raptu*, meaning *caught away or caught up*. This Latin word is equivalent to the Greek word *harpaze,* and is translated as *caught up* (1 Thessalonians 4:17). In 1 Thessalonians 4:14-18, the Apostle Paul states:

14For if we believe that Jesus died and rose again, even so them also which sleep in Jesus will God bring with him. 15For this we say unto you by the word of the Lord, that we which are alive and remain unto the coming of the Lord shall not prevent them which are asleep. 16For the Lord himself shall descend from heaven with a shout, with the voice of the archangel, and with the trump of God: and the dead in Christ shall rise first. 17Then we which are alive and remain shall be caught up together with them in the clouds, to meet the Lord in the air and so shall we ever be with the Lord. [18]Wherefore comfort one another with these words.

In this passage of scripture, the Apostle Paul comforts the people with the fact that those who had already died in Christ would not be prohibited from meeting the Lord when He called us. For those who do not believe the church will be raptured, let me pause to ask, why would Paul state this in scripture? Notice, the meeting will take place in the air.

If this is Jesus' second coming, it does not make sense for Him to call us to meet Him in the air, only to return to the Earth immediately thereafter. So what is Paul saying here? It is my belief, that with these scriptures, the Apostle Paul is confirming the removal of the church out of the Earth.

Let's examine the mystery or secret pertaining to the resurrection of the Body of Christ the Apostle Paul talked about in 1 Corinthians 15:51-52. It says:

"[51]Behold, I shew you a mystery; We shall not all sleep, but we shall all be changed, [52]In a moment, in the twinkling of an eye, at the last trump: for the

trumpet shall should, and the dead shall be raised incorruptible, and we shall be changed. For this corruptible must put on incorruption, and this mortal must put on immortality" (KJV).

When we examine these scriptures, we find that Paul is giving us a clue by using the word "*mystery*." By definition it means *secret*. In the preceding scripture, Paul was telling the Corinthians that everyone would not sleep or die. He explained that a secret was being revealed to them, that the day would come when the Body of Christ would experience a sudden change. Those who are God's children will receive glorified bodies; bodies that are incorruptible and immortal. Bodies that time would no longer ravage, and that would live forever. This sudden change is necessary for us to enter eternity and will take place when we are raptured away out of the Earth.

As of today, the church has yet to be caught up or raptured away but, at this point, we can all agree that this event will take place at some point in the future. What does the future look like? What is the purpose of Christ removing the church from the Earth, and more importantly, when will this event happen? There are three commonly discussed and highly debated views of the rapture within the church community. They are the pre-tribulation view, the mid-tribulation view, and the post-tribulation view. Let's take a moment to examine them.

Pre-Tribulation View

The pre-tribulation view is the belief that those who are believers in Jesus, will be raptured away before the start of the tribulation. This is the view I hold, based upon my research of the scriptures. Jesus spoke of certain signs to look for that would give us an idea of how close we are to His second coming. But why would He remove the Body of Christ before His return? Simply put, because of a promise given to us. Before Christ's second coming, the Almighty will pour out his wrath upon the Earth. The reasons for this will be discussed in a later chapter.

He promised the church that we would not have to experience His wrath. Is there scripture to prove this? Yes, there is. 1 Thessalonians 5:1-11 states:

"1But of the times and seasons, brethren, ye have no need that I write unto you. 2For yourselves know

perfectly that the day of the Lord so cometh as a thief in the night. 3For when they shall say, Peace and safety; then sudden destruction cometh upon them, as travail upon a woman with child; and they shall not escape. 4But ye, brethren, are not in darkness, that that day should overtake you as a thief. 5Ye are all the children of light, and the children of the day: we are not of the night, nor of darkness. 6Therefore let us not sleep, as do others; but let us watch and be sober. 7For they that sleep sleep in the night; and they that be drunken are drunken in the night. 8But let us, who are of the day, be sober, putting on the breastplate of faith and love; and for a helmet, the hope of salvation. 9For God hath not appointed us to wrath, but to obtain salvation by our Lord Jesus Christ. 10Who died for us, that, whether we wake or sleep, we should live together with him. 11Wherefore comfort yourselves together, and edify one another, even as also ye do" (KJV).

As we examine this passage of scripture, there are a couple of key words I need to point out. First, we need to understand that we are the children of light. The Bible says, God is a, *"lamp unto my feet, a light unto my path way." (Psalm 119:105).* As believers, we need to know His word because it helps us to know what He expects from us as it pertains to God's righteousness, peace, and joy in the Holy Ghost. Those who are in darkness are a people who do not have the Spirit of Christ in them. They may profess to be Christians, but their lives do not line up with the Word of God. Every tree is known by its fruit (Matthew 12:33).

Paul encourages believers to watch and be sober. The word *"watch."* In the Greek it means, *"to stay awake and keep watch".* Why are we told to stay awake? Is he saying not to go to sleep? Surely, that cannot be what this scripture means. Instead, Paul is admonishing us to pay close attention to the signs that are written in the Word of God regarding the return of Christ. Paul reminded the Thessalonians that the day of the Lord would, "come as a thief in the night," as a result, they needed to be ready at all times (1 Thessalonians 5:2).

How do we make ourselves ready? We do so by becoming born-again believers and living our lives consistent with the Word of God. "If any man be in Christ, he is a new creature" (2 Corinthians 5:17). There are some things I used to do that I don't do anymore, and there are places I used to go that I no longer go. In like manner, there are ways I used to think that I no longer think.

Paul also encouraged believers to be sober. The Greek word for sober means to, "abstain from wine; be sober; be discreet." Is Paul saying one cannot drink wine at all? No, I don't believe he is saying that, as he encourages Timothy to drink a little wine for the stomach's sake (1Timothy 5:23). The Israelites were known to drink wine, and Christ also turned water into wine. I don't believe Paul is saying that but we should understand that being a drunkard is strongly prohibited (Isaiah 22:13; John 2:1-11; Proverbs 23:19:20).

Paul also informed the Thessalonians that God has not, "appointed us to wrath." Instead, He has, "given us the promise to obtain salvation through Jesus Christ" (1 Thessalonians 5:9). He will do this by rapturing away the Body of Christ before the start of the Tribulation Period. It is here that we see, God's plan is not for us to suffer the wrath that will be poured out upon the earth during the Tribulation Period.

On this Christian journey, there are many who attend

church and profess Christianity. However, it is my fear that many will be left behind and forced to experience the wrath of God, as it is poured out on the world. Why do I fear this? Because many fail to follow the commands of God; taking the grace of God for granted. Some believe that because we are under grace, our lives can continue to be filled with sin and unrighteousness. This is just not the case. We are called to be a holy people, set apart from the world (1 Peter 2:9). Christ Jesus taught that not everyone who says Lord, would enter into His kingdom. He goes on to say, "many will say in that day, we cast out devils in your name, and prophesied in your name, yet I will say unto them I never knew you; depart from me ye workers of iniquity" (Matthew 7: 21-23).

When Christ Jesus walked the Earth, before His crucifixion, He admonished believers to live our lives in such a way that we were always prepared to meet Him, as we are unaware of the time of His return. In the Gospel of Luke 21, Jesus shared signs we should watch for in expectation of His second coming and concerning escaping His wrath.

"34And take heed to yourselves, lest at any time your

hearts be overcharged with surfeiting, and drunkenness, and care of this life, and so that day come upon you unawares. 35For as a snare shall it come on all them that dwell on the face of the whole earth. 36Watch ye therefore, and pray always, that ye may be accounted worthy to escape all these things that shall come to pass, and to stand before the Son of man."

Luke 21:34-36 (KJV)

Christ Jesus admonished believers not to be caught up with the cares of this world, yet believers all over the world have become consumed with all the distractions of life. The lust of the flesh and the pride of life, will ultimately cause many to be left behind and forced to experience the wrath of God. What then should we be doing? We should be doing exactly what Christ said, "watching and praying always."

The wrath, which is to come upon the world, is seriously dire. We need to always be in prayer, so that we might escape the things that are to come. The Greek word *escape* means, *"to go, to flee out, escape, flee."* A reference found in Strong's Concordance #5343 also has a meaning that says, *"to vanish, to escape, flee away."*

This definition of the word *"vanish,"* references back to 1 Thessalonians 4:17. If we vanish, then where shall we appear? We will meet Him in the air when we are raptured.

When will the rapture take place? A clue to the timing is noted in a scripture we previously discussed. In 1 Corinthians 15:52, Paul tells us we would all be changed at the last trump. I do not expect many Christians to understand the terminology used here. In order to understand the significance of the phrase the *"last trump,"* one would need to be familiar with the seven feasts of the Lord found in Leviticus 23:1-44.

God commanded the Israelites to observe the holy feasts. The seven feasts of the Lord were the Passover, the Feast of Unleavened Bread, the Feast of First-Fruits, the Feast of Pentecost, the Feast of Trumpets, the Day of Atonement, and the Feast of Tabernacles.

Christ was crucified on the Passover, buried on the day of unleavened bread, and rose again on the day of the Feast of First-Fruits. Fifty days later, on the day of the Feast of Pentecost, God poured out his Spirit upon the believers who were gathered in the upper room (Acts 2). During the Feast of Trumpets, the trumpet would be blown at various times. Some scholars believe the Jews of today celebrate this feast by blowing a trumpet a total of one-hundred times with that last blow of the trumpet being called the last trump. Paul made it clear that our change would occur at the "last trump," so this has a significant meaning for the Body of Christ.

An additional clue that the rapture will occur during the feast of trumpets is found in Joel 2:15-16. It reads:

"15Blow the trumpet in Zion, sanctify a fast, call a solemn assembly; 16Gather the people, sanctify the congregation, assemble the elders, gather the children, and those that suck the breast: let the bridegroom go forth of his chamber, and the bride out of her closet."

In the preceding verses, Joel sees the coming wrath of God being poured out on the Earth (Joel 2:1-14). He then gives a clue, beginning in verse 15, with the blowing of the trumpet, and calling for a solemn assembly. The solemn assembly is connected to the seven feasts of the Lord, and the blowing of the trumpet is what starts the feast of trumpets.

In verses 16 and 17, proceeding the blowing of the trumpet, the bride; symbolic of the biblical church, and the bridegroom; symbolic of Jesus, meet. This is a picture of the rapture.

As I conclude this section, let it be noted that the answers to any remaining questions can be found in the book of Revelation; this book holds the key to unveiling the future. What we learn will give us a better understanding as to how the future will unfold. If anyone chose to discredit the book of Revelation and its relevance, they would never come to understand God's plan for mankind. The prophetic message of this book is communicated through dramatic apocalyptic images and symbolisms. When John received this prophetic revelation, he told us that we are to, "keep those things which are written in this book for the time is at hand" (Revelation 1:3). Some have misinterpreted this scripture, as a result, they are excluding all future events.

The key to understanding how these future events will unfold is found in Revelation 1:19. It reads, "write the things which thou hast seen, and the things which are, and the things which shall be hereafter." In this verse,

John was informed that the revelations he had received from verses 1-18 were considered past, and that the things which he was about to see in verse 20, and in chapters 2-3 of Revelation would, at that time, be the present.

When we examine the seven letters written to the seven churches in Revelation 2 and 3, we get a picture of how they relate to the unfolding of future events. By addressing the churches, Christ was revealing to John that He would be addressing the church; a prepared people. It is not until Revelation 4 that things shift, but before expounding on the relevance of Revelation 4, we need to discuss Revelation 3:7-10. It reads:

"7And unto the angel of the church in Philadelphia write; These things saith he that is holy, he that is true, he that hath the key to David, he that openeth, and no man shutteth, and shutteth, and no man openeth. 8I know thy works: behold, I have set before thee an open door, and no man can shut it: for thou hast a little strength, and hast kept my word, and hast not denied my name. 9Behold, I will make them of the synagogue of Satan, which say they are Jews, and are not, but do lie; behold, I mill make them to

come and worship before thy feet, and to know that I have loved thee. ¹⁰Because thou hast kept the word of my patience, I also will keep them from the hour of temptation, which shall come upon the world, to try them that dwell upon the earth."

What is the hour of temptation that Christ promised to keep the church of Philadelphia from? How was He going to fulfill that promise? The hour of temptation is the wrath of God being poured out on the entire world. God set before the church of Philadelphia an open door that no man was able to shut. He did this, because this church represented a people, who were living a lifestyle pleasing to Christ. Their reward was them escaping the coming tribulation the rest of the world would experience. How would He fulfill His promise to them?

A description and explanation is found in 1Thessalonians 4:16-17.

"¹⁶For the Lord himself shall descend from heaven with a shout, with the voice of the archangel, and with the trump of God: and the dead in Christ shall rise first: ¹⁷*Then we which are alive and remain shall be caught up together with them in the clouds, to*

meet the Lord in the air: and so shall we ever be with the Lord."

To effectively expound on the "*hereafter*" found in Revelation 1:19, we must look at Revelation 4:1 to obtain an explanation of what the "*hereafter*" is.

"After this I looked, and, behold, a door was opened in heaven: and the first voice which I heard was as it were of a trumpet talking with me; which said, Come up hither, and I will shew thee things which must be hereafter."

The question arises. . . after what? After the church is removed out of the Earth. As we examine this verse, we see that the Apostle John heard the sound of a trumpet, then a door was opened in Heaven. A voice called to him instructing him to, "come up hither" so he could be shown the things which had to take place thereafter. As we read this verse and the ones following, notice how the scene immediately shifts from the churches on Earth, to Heaven.

In Revelation 4:2, we see that John was immediately moved in the spirit and stood before the throne of the Almighty God. He goes on to describe the appearance of

23

the throne and reveals the twenty-four elders, who were clothed in white raiment with crowns of gold upon their heads. Who are those twenty-four elders? The elders represent the Old Testament twelve tribes of Israel and the twelve Apostles of the Lamb. This would incorporate both the Old Testament saints who were deemed worthy to appear before the throne of God, as well as the New Testament church.

In Revelation 4:10-11, the twenty-four elders were worshiping and praising the Almighty God. It is important to note, as they worshipped, they cast their crowns before the throne and gave praise to God. It is important to know that the believers along with the elders already have their rewards; their crowns. This means they were at the judgment seat of Christ. The Apostle Paul told the Corinthians about this in 1 Corinthians 3:13-15:

"13Every man's work shall be made manifest: for the day shall declare it, because it shall be revealed by fire; and the fire shall try every man's work or what sort it is. 14If any man's work abide which he hath built thereupon, he shall receive a reward. 15If any

man's work shall be burned, he shall suffer loss: but he himself shall be saved; yet so as by fire."

Having their crowns in their possession to cast before the throne of God, solidifies their heavenly presence. Need further proof? Revelation 5 begins with the Almighty God sitting on the throne holding a book in His right hand. This book is of great importance because it contains revelations of what God has determined to happen to humanity in the future. We see that a strong angel proclaims with a loud voice, "Who is worthy to open the book, and to loose the seals thereof?" We find there is none worthy except the Lamb of God. The seals referenced, are the first seven of twenty-one judgments that will be set upon the earth. The opening of the first seal will start the seven-year Tribulation Period, also known as the wrath of God (Revelation 6:16).

There are two importance things to note here; the bride is in Heaven, and the "wrath of God" has not yet been unleashed. Revelation 5:8-12 gives us further confirmation of this:

"8And when he had taken the book, the four beasts and four and twenty elders fell down before the Lamb, having every one of them harps, and golden

vials full of odours, which are the prayers of saints.
⁹And they sung a new song, saying, Thou art worthy
to take the book, and to open the seals thereof: for
thou wast slain, and hast redeemed us to God by thy
blood out of every kindred, and tongue, and people,
and nation; ¹⁰And hast made us unto our God kings
and priests: and we shall reign on the earth. ¹¹And I
beheld, and I heard the voice of many angels round
about the throne and the beasts and the elders: and
the number of them was ten thousand times ten
thousand, and thousands of thousands; ¹²Saying
with a loud voice, Worthy is the Lamb that was slain
to receive power, and riches, and wisdom, and
strength, and honour, and glory, and blessing."

Verse 9, shows us that those gathered are praising God
and singing a new song. It goes on to share how God
redeemed those who were present by His blood, and
references the diversity of the crowd as every kindred,
tongue, people, and nation. Verse 11 gives us a picture
of the diversity and of those gathered, and of the
multitude of saints who are gathered at the throne.
These are the Old Testament saints as well as the New
Testament church. Both are standing before the throne

of God, prior to the wrath of God being released upon the Earth.

It is my assignment to prepare a people to escape what is about to come upon the Earth. I admonish all believers to prepare to meet Christ. He is soon to come, and will remove His bride, the church, out of the Earth, prior to releasing His wrath upon the Earth.

Mid-Tribulation View

The second view I'd like us to examine is the mid-tribulation view. This view, more commonly held, holds to the belief that the church will be raptured during the middle of the seven-year Tribulation Period, or 3½ years into it. Many who argue this view try to piece together certain scriptures to support their ideology and philosophy.

When studying eschatology, one needs to allow the scriptures to fit exactly where they must go. We must never take scriptures out of context. When we do, it causes us to have a false view. It is our job to ensure that we are rightly dividing the Word of truth. Let's take a look at the scriptures many used to try and push this false narrative. 2 Thessalonians 2:1-12 reads:

"1Now we beseech you, brethren, by the coming of our Lord Jesus Christ, and by our gathering together unto him, 2That ye be not shaken in mind, or be troubled, neither by spirit, nor by word, nor by letter as from us, as that the day of Christ is at hand. 3Let no man deceive you by any means: for that day shall not come, except there come a falling away first, and that man of sin be revealed, the son of perdition; 4Who opposeth and exalteth himself above all that is called God, or that is worshipped; so that he as God sitteth in the temple of God, shewing himself that he is God. 5Remember ye not, that, when I was yet with you, I told you these things? 6And now ye know what withholdeth that he might be revealed in this time. 7For the mystery of iniquity doth already work: only he who now letteth will let, until he be taken out of the way. 8And then shall that Wicked be revealed, whom the Lord shall consume with the spirit of his mouth, and shall destroy with the brightness of his coming: 9Even him, whose coming is after the working of Satan with all power and signs and lying

wonders, 10And with deceivableness of unrighteousness in them that perish; because they received not the love of the truth, that they might be saved. 11And for this cause God shall send them strong delusion, that they should believe a lie: 12That they all might be damned who believed not the truth, but had pleasure in unrighteousness."

Those who hold to this view, attempt to use verses one and three to establish their point. They fail to recognize, when Paul writes this letter to them, he uses the words in this chapter because he had already told them they would be caught up to meet the Lord in the air in 1 Thessalonians 4. He had already assured them they would escape the wrath that was to come. False teachers crept in, and began teaching the people that the day of the Lord had already begun. They lead the people to believe God's final wrath was already being poured out on the Earth. This was not true. Paul began educating them. He shared that there were a couple of things which had to take place before the wrath of God was going to be poured out.

First, there had to come the falling away. The Greek word falling away is "*apostasia*" (Strong's Concordance

#646). It means departure, or abandonment. In the last days, many who profess Christ will not have lifestyles that are consistent with the Word of God. Many will depart from or abandon holiness; the set apart lifestyle God requires of us. "It is written be *holy for I am holy*; *follow peace with all men, holiness without which, no man shall see the Lord"* (1 Peter 1:16; Hebrews 12:14).

People will depart from sound teaching which requires separation from the world and a sinful lifestyle. In an attempt to maintain membership, some church leaders will offer "cheap grace," but we must make every effort not to fall into that category. We must endeavor to be like the five wise virgins, and maintain lamps full of oil. The second thing Paul shared was that the man of sin had to be revealed. This world ruler will be restrained. His true identity and activity will be hidden until God permits his rule to begin.

I believe God will restrain him until after the bride, the church, is removed out of the Earth. Why do I believe this? As long as the church is present, the ability for the Antichrist to deceive the world regarding his identity will not possible. With the church present, he will not be able to disguise himself as someone simply seeking peace.

Believers in Christ are given *dunamis* (Greek) power (Acts 1:8). This gives believers authority to drive out evil spirits and heal the sick in Jesus name. We have been given keys to the kingdom and delegated authority to bind and loose. So, when the church is removed, all this power will leave with the church. Although the Holy Spirit will still be on earth, His power will be used by the two prophets mentioned in Revelation 11:3-8. Some also contend that the Holy Spirit will also empower the 144,000 sealed Israelites foretold in Revelation 7:3-8.

Once again, the mid-tribulation view maintains that the church will be removed three and half years into the seven-year tribulation. Those who accept this view believe the wrath of God will not be poured out until the opening of the sixth seal, as mentioned in Revelation 6:12-17. The problem with this argument is that there is no solid scriptural proof to support this theory; except, as mentioned earlier, what some individuals attempt to piece together.

Some mid-tribulation believers attempt to use Revelation 7:4, 9-17 to support their argument of this view. Let's look at these verses.

"⁴And I heard the number of them which were sealed: and there were sealed an hundred and forty and four thousand of all the tribes of the children of Israel. ⁹After this I beheld, and, lo, a great multitude, which no man could number, of all nations, and kindreds, and people, and tongues, stood before the throne, and before the Lamb, clothed with white robes, and palms in their hands; ¹⁰And cried with a loud voice, saying Salvation to our God which sitteth upon the throne, and unto the Lamb. ¹¹And all the angels stood round about the throne, and about the elders and the four beasts, and fell before the throne on their faces, and worshipped God, ¹²Saying, Amen: Blessing, and glory, and wisdom, and thanksgiving, and honour, and power, and might, be unto our God for ever and ever. Amen. ¹³And one of the elders answered, saying unto me, What are these which are arrayed in white robes? And whence came they? ¹⁴And I said unto him, Sir, thou knowest. And he said to me, These are they which came out of great tribulation, and have

washed their robes, and made them white in the blood of the Lamb. 15Therefore are they before the throne of God, and serve him day and night in his temple: and he that sitteth on the throne shall dwell among them. 16They shall hunger no more, neither thirst any more; neither shall the sun light on them, nor any heat. 17For the Lamb which is in the midst of the throne shall feed them, and shall lead them unto living fountains of waters: and God shall wipe away all tears from their eyes."

As explained in these verses, before the seventh seal is opened, 144,000 Israelites are sealed in their foreheads. These Israelites will be used to evangelize Christ to the world, but will largely target the lost tribes of Israel who have been scattered all over the world. In Revelation 7:9, we see there is a great number of people standing before the throne. The Israelites, whose eyes were blinded to Jesus being the Messiah, will come to the realization of who He is, and will return to Him in great numbers.

During a conversation the Apostle John had with an elder at the throne, he is told that those arrayed in white robes have come out of the Great Tribulation.

This verse alone completely discredits the mid-tribulation view as the Great Tribulation does not start until Revelation 13 with the unveiling of the Antichrist, followed by his forty-two-month rule. This time of great distress, also referred to as Jacob's trouble, is described in Jeremiah 30:7.

As you read the book of Revelation, you will see that there is no proof nor mention of the church on Earth during any of the Tribulation Period. After Revelation 3, the church is not mentioned until the end of the book of Revelation in chapter 22.

Post-Tribulation View

Lastly, we will discuss the post-tribulation view. According to those who hold this view, the church will be present on the Earth for the entire duration of the seven-year tribulation. However, as we look into the scriptures, it will be shown that there is no sound evidence to support this view. The argument used doesn't make sense at all. My reason for saying this is because those who believe in the post-tribulation view, discredit all the scriptures present in the Word of God, which point to the deliverance of the church from the impending wrath of God.

The things spoken by Christ concerning His second coming are totally ignored in this view, but we know that God has always provided a way of escape for those who are obedient to Him. As an example, in Noah's day, only eight people escaped the flood by way of the ark, while everyone else perished; both the old and the young (babies included). Those who perished refused to heed the words and warnings preached by Noah for centuries. They refused to change and as a result were left behind to suffer the wrath of God.

Another reference is the story of Sodom and Gomorrah. Lot and his family heeded the words of the angels which were to warn them. They were instructed to escape the city as its destruction was imminent. Initially, everyone was obedient to the servants of God, and their lives were spared. However, although she came very close, Lot's wife did not receive the salvation that was afforded to her because she turned and looked back. This will be the story of many in the body of Christ. When the rapture comes, many will get so close to being counted in the number, but will faint and turn back in the days just prior to.

Like the mid-tribulation view, there are a number of scriptures, some used out of context, in an attempt to prove this ideology. One of the scriptures inaccurately used by post-tribulation believers in an attempt to solidify their belief is Matthew 24:29-31. It reads: *29Immediately after the tribulation of those days shall the sun be darkened, and the moon shall not give her light, and the stars shall fall from heaven, and the powers of the heavens shall be shaken: 30And then shall appear the sign of the Son of man in heaven: and then shall all the tribes of the earth mourn, and they shall see the Son of man coming in the clouds of heaven with power and great glory. 31And he shall send his angels with a great sound of a trumpet, and they shall gather together his elect from the four winds, from one end of heaven to the other.*

Those who hold to this view, take Christ's statements regarding His return to Earth, immediately after the tribulation, which is the second coming, as proof that those events are the rapture. Jesus will send His angels with a great sound of a trumpet, and the angels will gather His elect from the four winds, and one end of Heaven to the other, but what they fail to understand is that those being gathered from the four corners of the Earth are the ones who made it through the seven-year Tribulation Period. Notice there is nothing said about this group of people being changed, in a moment, in a twinkling of an eye. Also notice that there is no meeting the Lord in the air. Instead, they are gathered by angels.

The question now becomes, if the church has already been raptured during the pre-tribulation period, then who are the elect being gathered in verse 31? Those being gathered by the angels during this time are the scattered Israelites who survived the Tribulation Period, as previously mentioned in this chapter.

Remember, the Tribulation Period is centered on the Israelites coming to the realization that Jesus is the Messiah, and coming back into covenant with Him. The gathering from the four winds, from one end of Heaven to another is necessary as this group of people have been scattered all over the Earth. God will fulfill the promises He made in Ezekiel 37:13-14, and in Isaiah

11:12. He will restore them back to their homeland both physically and spiritually.

"13And ye shall know that I am the Lord, when I have opened your graves, O my people, and brought you up out of your graves, 14And shall put my spirit in you, and ye shall live, and I shall place you in your own land: then shall ye know that I the Lord have spoken it, and performed it, saith the Lord.

Ezekiel 37:13-14 (KJV)

12And he shall set up an ensign for the nations, and shall assemble the outcast of Israel, and gather together the dispersed of Judah from the four corners of the earth."

Isaiah 11:12 (KJV)

A final scripture, post-tribulation viewers use to support their view is Revelation 20:4-5. It reads:

"4And I saw thrones, and they sat upon them, and judgment was given unto them: and I saw the souls of them that were beheaded for the witness of Jesus, and for the word of God, and which had not worshipped the beast, neither his image, neither had

received his mark upon their foreheads, or in their hands; and they lived and reigned with Christ a thousand years. ⁵But the rest of the dead lived not again until the thousand years were finished. This is the first resurrection."

If we allow the scriptures to speak for themselves, it is clear who was being resurrected at this time. These are the people who died during the Tribulation Period. This is known because the scriptures clearly speak about, and singles out those who had been beheaded for being a witness of Jesus and who had not received the mark of the beast.

Once again, notice that there is no sudden change, no meeting Jesus in the air, and no sounding of the trumpet for those who are dead to be raised up. If we allow the scriptures to speak for themselves, it is clear what the future holds as it pertains to the rapture of the church.

⌘ CHAPTER TWO ⌘

Daniel's 70th Week

The 70th week of Daniel is crucial to eschatology. We are going to start with an overview of what it is and discuss why it is so crucial when it comes to the future of mankind.

In Daniel 9:2, he acknowledged and understood that after seventy years of captivity, Judah would be restored to their homeland. He had this understanding because he had read books which were written by prophets.

Daniel was very concerned at that time. The end of the seventy years was quickly approaching, yet the people of Israel experienced no change to their current predicament. Daniel sought the Lord through prayer and supplication in order to gain understanding of what was going on. One of the reasons I believe he was troubled is because he believed the words of the prophets; he knew they could not lie.

The prophet Jeremiah spoke of restoration for the children of Israel after seventy years (Jeremiah 25:11-

12). At this time, it appeared as if it was not going to happen. However, while Daniel, the prophet, was praying and confessing, both his sins and the sins of the people, the angel Gabriel interrupted him and began speaking to him concerning his people.

"24Seventy weeks are determined upon thy people and upon thy holy city, to finish the transgression, and to make an end of sins, and to make reconciliation for iniquity, and to bring in everlasting righteousness, and to seal up the vision and prophecy, and to anoint the most Holy. 25Know therefore and understand, that from the going forth of the commandment to restore and to build Jerusalem unto the Messiah the Prince shall be seven weeks, and threescore and two weeks: the street shall be built again, and the wall, even in troublous times. 26And after threescore and two weeks shall Messiah be cut off, but not for himself: and the people of the prince that shall come shall destroy the city and the sanctuary; and the end thereof shall be with a flood, and unto the end of the war desolations are determined. 27And he shall confirm the covenant with many for one week: and in the midst of the week

he shall cause the sacrifice and the oblation to cease,
and for the overspreading of abominations he shall
make it desolate, even until the consummation, and
that determined shall be poured upon the desolate."

Daniel 9:24-27(KJV)

Let's discuss these scriptures to get an understanding of what they are referring to. God revealed to Daniel that He would use a total of seventy weeks, 490 years, or seventy, seven-year periods to deal with the people of Judah and Israel. It is important to understand that when God says "His people," to Daniel, He is not referring to the church or the gentiles. Instead, God is speaking of the whole House of Israel. Who is the House of Israel? They are descendants of the twelve tribes of Jacob, whose name was changed to Israel back in Genesis 32:28. It is important to understand who the Lord is referring to when He is speaking to Daniel, because the Israelites, and God's chronological order in dealing with them, is critical to unlocking and understanding future events.

Let's take a look at the numbers revealed to Daniel in these scriptures. Gabriel tells Daniel, that sixty-nine of the seventy weeks, a total of 483 years, would pass between the time of the commandment to restore and rebuild Jerusalem until the Messiah. However, when the Messiah was crucified or "cut off" as it is put in scripture, that stopped the passage of the remaining seven years or one week needed to conclude the seventy weeks. With the sixty-nine weeks already behind us, we will now discuss those numbers and start dates.

Verse 27, gives us a revelation of when the 70th week, or the remaining 7-year period will start. The remaining time will start when he, the Antichrist, confirms the covenant (peace treaty) with many, including the Nation of Israel for 1 week or 7 years. This 1 week or 7-year period is referred to as the Tribulation Period; with the last 3½ years being referred to as the Great Tribulation.

The Apostle Paul made reference to this event in 1 Thessalonians 5:3 saying, "For when they shall say, peace and safety; then sudden destruction cometh upon them, as travail upon a woman with child; and they shall not escape."

The Antichrist will come in the name of peace, causing many people to believe in him. As a result, he will be able to accomplish that which no one else before him was able to. He will have the ability to negotiate peace agreements and covenants between the nation of Israel and their enemies.

However, Daniel is informed that in the middle of the treaty, (after forty-two months), the Antichrist will break his agreement by going into the rebuilt temple and declaring himself to be God. This will be the sign to the children of Israel that Jacob's trouble, as mentioned in Jeremiah 30:7, has begun. Jesus made reference of this event in Matthew 24:15-21. It reads:

"15When ye therefore shall see the abomination of desolation, spoken of by Daniel the prophet, stand in the holy place, (whoso readeth, let him understand:) 16Then let them which be in Judaea flee into the mountains: 17Let him which is on the housetop not come down to take any thing out of his house: 18Neither let him which is in the field return back to take his clothes. 19And woe unto them that are with child, and to them that give suck in those days! 20But pray ye that your flight be not in the winter, neither

on the sabbath day: ²¹For then shall be great tribulation, such as was not since the beginning of the world to this time, no, nor ever shall be."

In this passage of scripture, Jesus Christ confirms the words spoken by the prophet Daniel. Both were able to see these future events and revealed them in their writings to ensure the people of God were aware and not caught sleeping. Regardless of what other eschatology teachers may say, the fact of the matter is, these things have not yet happened, but will occur in the near future. One week, or one seven-year period remains in the prophecy and we will soon witness the fulfillment of it.

My heart goes out to the Twelve tribes of Israel; those who are scattered all over the world and who have yet to make Jesus Christ their Messiah. What is coming during the 70th week of Daniel's prophecy, also known as, "Jacob's trouble" will be a time of tribulation and great tribulation, such has never been seen or experienced before. Those left on the Earth following the Rapture can only maintain hope in God's promise that a remnant will be saved.

⌘ CHAPTER THREE ⌘

The Seven-Year Tribulation

What is the Tribulation Period? I am certain this is one of the major questions in both your heart and mind. The church has discussed both the rapture of the church and the coming tribulation period for centuries. Even those who are not skilled in eschatology have some knowledge of this future event. In eschatology, the word *"tribulation"* is only referenced four times in the New Testament.

The Greek word **"tribulation"** means *pressure (literally or figuratively), afflicted, anguish, burdened, persecution, tribulation, trouble.* Believers of Christ have always experienced situations which presented pressure, afflictions, burdens and persecutions; many have found themselves in an abundance of trouble.

To review, when we speak of the Tribulation or the Tribulation Period, we are referring to the 70th week of Daniel; as discussed in the previous chapter. This 70th week is a 7-year period which God will use to deal with His chosen people, the nation of Israel. It will begin when the man of sin, the son of perdition, also known as

47

the Antichrist, organizes a 7-year agreement with many nations. This will be the beginning of the Tribulation Period.

Although Jesus Christ spoke about the afflictions that would await the Israelites during the tribulation in Matthew 24:15-35 and in Mark 13:24-26, the book of Revelation is needed to gain a clear understanding of what it will look like in full detail. In Revelation 4, the church has already been taken up into Heaven via the Rapture and Revelation 5, begins with God Almighty holding a book in His hand as He sits on the throne. Christ Jesus, our Lord, is pictured here symbolically, as the Lion of the Tribe of Judah and as the Lamb who was slain for the sins of the world.

The information contained in this book can be described as the twenty-one judgments of God that will be poured out on the Earth. Each of these judgments will unleash a great deal of affliction and punishment. The twenty-one judgments will come in three sets of seven. The first seven are the seal judgments, the second seven are the trumpet judgments, and the third seven are known as the bowl judgments.

As we read in Revelation 5, we see that Christ is the only one worthy to open the book and unleash His wrath. Revelation 6 begins with Jesus opening the seals that are in the book.

"**1And I saw when the Lamb opened one of the seals, and I heard, as it were the noise of thunder, one of the four beasts saying, Come and see.**

2And I saw, and behold a white horse: and he that sat on him had a bow; and a crown was given unto him: and he went forth conquering, and to conquer. 3And when he had opened the second seal, I heard the second beast say, Come and see. 4And there went out another horse that was red: and power was given to him that sat thereon to take peace from the earth, and that they should kill one another: and there was given unto him a great sword. 5And when he had opened the third seal, I head the third beast say, Come and see. And I beheld, and lo a black horse; and he that sat on him had a pair of balances in his hand. 6And I heard a voice in the midst of the four beasts say, A measure of wheat for a penny, and three measures of barley for a penny; and see thou hurt not the oil and the wine. 7And when he had opened the fourth seal, I heard the voice of the fourth beast say, Come and see. ⁸And I looked and behold a pale horse: and his name that sat on him was Death, and Hell followed with him. And the power was given unto them over the fourth part of the earth, to kill with sword, and with hunger, and with death, and with the beast of the earth."

Revelation 6:1-8

These verses give us a picture of four horsemen being released upon the Earth. As the first seal is opened, it releases God's judgment upon the systems of this evil and wicked world. The rider of the white horse is a symbol of the Antichrist, operating as a world ruler. After his role in negotiating the signing of a treaty with many nations, the Antichrist is initially looked upon as a world leader, who was able to bring world peace. His true identity and intentions are revealed 3½ years, or 42 months into the tribulation period.

Once his true identity and intentions are revealed, he will begin to wreak havoc upon the world for the remaining forty-two months of his reign. It is important to note that the Tribulation Period does not start until the signing of the peace treaty. The Rapture will occur, removing the church from the Earth, but there is no biblical basis that says the Tribulation Period will start the next day. Imagine the world, and the chaos that will ensue, as millions of people simply disappear. Drivers will disappear from behind the wheel of their cars, causing major accidents. Pilots will disappear from the cockpit of the planes they are flying, causing planes to fall from the sky. Missiles will accidentally be launched, and boats will collide, all because their operators have vanished with the rapture of the church.

The need for peace and for someone to assist with picking up the pieces to get the world moving again will be imperative. This is how the Antichrist will come in and be able to deceive so many.

The second horseman, riding upon a red horse, is given power to take peace from the Earth, causing men to kill one another. When these afflictions begin, people in the world will be so unprepared. They will not understand why they are suddenly filled with hate and violence towards their fellow man.

The third horseman, who will be riding upon a black horse, will have the responsibility of causing famine to sweep the land. Basic necessities of life will not only be scarce, but the cost of those necessities will be exorbitant and will result in widespread starvation.

The fourth horseman, riding upon a pale horse, is identified as "Death," the Bible says, "and hell followed with him." This is a point where things will hit a new height of war, famine, plagues, diseases, and death. As a result of all this activity, ¼ of all people living, will die.

When Christ opens the fifth seal, the people in Heaven, under the altar, who had been slain for the Word of God, and for the testimony which they kept, are noted as crying with a loud voice, seeking vengeance against those who spilled their blood and took their lives. They are given white robes and told to rest for a season, as their fellow brethren would be killed as they were (Revelation 6:9-11).

When Christ opens the sixth seal, darkness and numerous natural disasters will flood the earth. There will be enormous pain, sorrow, suffering, and torment for everyone, rich, poor, bond, and free. So much so, that men will beg for and seek death, only to be denied it.

Before the seventh seal is opened, an angel is dispatched with the responsibility to seal the 144,000 Israelites who will be sent to the Nation of Israel; those who are scattered throughout the four corners of the Earth. Their duty will be to preach the Gospel of Jesus Christ to them in an effort to turn them back to God.

As a result of their evangelistic work, millions will be saved during the Great Tribulation. The purpose of sealing them at this point is to protect them from the impending trumpet and bowl judgments, which are set to be released on the Earth. In addition, it will serve to protect them from the demonic activity which will be occurring on Earth, during that time.

The opening of the seventh seal, initiates the seven trumpet judgments which are next to be poured out on the Earth. Each of these seven trumpet judgments, will unleash a part of God's wrath, causing great loss of life on the Earth. Revelation 8:1-12 reads:

"¹And when he had opened the seventh seal, there was silence in heaven about the space of half an hour. ²And I saw the seven angels which stool before God; and to them were given seven trumpets. ³And

another angel came and stood at the altar, having a golden censer; and there was given unto him much incense, that he should offer it with the prayers of all saints upon the golden altar which was before the throne. 4And the smoke of the incense, which came with the prayers of the saints, ascended up before God out of the angel's hand. 5And the angel took the censer, and filled it with fire of the altar, and cast it into the earth: and there were voices, and thundering, and lightnings, and an earthquake. 6And the seven angels which had the seven trumpets prepared themselves to sound. 7The first angel sounded, and there followed hail and fire mingled with blood, and they were cast upon the earth: and the third part of threes was burnt up, and all green grass was burnt up. 8And the second angel sounded, and as it were a great mountain burning with fire was cast into the sea: and the third part of the sea became blood; 9And the third part of the creatures which were in the sea, and had life, died; and the third part of the ships were destroyed. 10And the third angel sounded, and there fell a great star from heaven, burning as it were a lamp, and it fell upon the third part of the rivers, and upon the fountains of waters; 11And the name of the star is called Wormwood: and the third part of the waters became wormwood; and many men died of the waters, because they were made bitter. 12And the fourth angel sounded, and the third part of the sun was smitten, and the third part of the moon, and the third part of the stars; so as the third part of the them was darkened, and the day shone not for a third part of it, and the night likewise."

As the first four trumpet judgments begin, one third of the Earth's crops are destroyed by fire and hail, one third of the sea and river is polluted, and the sun, moon, and stars are darkened for a third part of the day and night. These judgments of the Lord, will cause a great deal of destruction both on the Earth and to human life. With the last three trumpet judgments, as described in Revelation 9, and in Revelation 10:1-7, we see that the intensity of the judgments continues to increase.

We must also keep in mind that all the trumpet judgments will occur in the middle of the first forty-two months of the Tribulation Period. Revelation 9 reads:

"¹And the fifth angel sounded, and I saw a star fall from heaven unto the earth: and to him was given the key of the bottomless pit. ²And he opened the bottomless pit; and there arose a smoke out of the pit, as the smoke of a great furnace; and the sun and the air were darkened by reason of the smoke of the pit. ³And there came out of the smoke locusts upon the earth: and unto them was given power, as the scorpions of the earth have power. ⁴And it was commanded them that they should not hurt the grass of the earth, neither any green thing, neither any tree; but only those men which have not the seal of God in their foreheads. ⁵And to them it was given that they should not kill them, but that they should be tormented five months: and their torment was as the torment of a scorpion, when he striketh a man. ⁶And in those days shall men seek death, and shall not find it; and shall desire to die, and death shall flee from them. ⁷And the shapes of the locusts were like unto horses prepared unto battle; and on their heads were as it were crowns like gold, and their faces were as the faces of men. ⁸And they had hair as the hair of women, and their teeth were as the teeth of lions. ⁹And they had breastplates, as it were breastplates of

iron; and the sound of their wings was as the sound of chariots of many horses running to battle. ¹⁰And they had tails like unto scorpions, and there were stings in their tails: and their power was to hurt men five months. ¹¹And they had a king over them, which is the angel of the bottomless pit, whose name in the Hebrew tongue is Abaddon, but in the Greek tongue hath his name Apollyon. ¹²One woe is past; and, behold, there come two woes more hereafter. ¹³And the sixth angel sounded, and I heard a voice from the four horns of the golden altar which is before God,

¹⁴Saying to the sixth angel which had the trumpet, Loose the four angels which are bound in the great river Euphrates. *¹⁵And the four angels were loosed, which were prepared for an hour, and a day, and a month, and a year, for to slay the third part of men. ¹⁶And the number of the army of the horsemen were two hundred thousand thousand: and I heard the number of them. ¹⁷And thus I saw the horses in the vision, and them that sat on them, having breastplates of fire, and of jacinth, and brimstone: and the heads of the horses were as the heads of lions; and out of their mouths issued fire and smoke and brimstone. ¹⁸By these three was the third part of* *men killed, by the fire, and by the smoke, and by the brimstone, which issued out of their mouths. ¹⁹For their power is in their mouth, and in their tails: for their tails were like unto serpents, and had heads, and with them they do hurt. ²⁰And the rest of the men which were not killed by these plagues yet repented not of the works of their hands, that they should not worship devils, and idols of gold, and silver, and brass, and stone, and of wood: which neither can see, nor hear, nor walk: ²¹Neither repented they of their murders, nor of their sorceries, nor of their fornication, nor of their thefts."*

The fifth trumpet brings about a great number of locusts, which is symbolic of demons and demonic activity being released upon the Earth. Their purpose is to torment those on Earth for a period of five months. Again, the pain and suffering will be so great, that people will want to die, but won't be able to.

The six trumpet begins with the unleashing of a massive army of horsemen lead by four angels which are all specifically prepared for this time. Scholars differ on their theories concerning the makeup of this army. Some believe they may be evil angels or even demons, while others believe they are mounted troops; representing many armies gathered for battle. When they are released, they will cause the death of one third of those alive on Earth. Even with all the pain and horrors occurring, the men of the Earth will harden their hearts toward God, rather than before Him,

Revelation 9:20-21 addresses those who were not killed by the plagues. It reads, "they repented not of the works of their hands, their idol worship, their devil worship," etc. This verse continues to list a number of other things including, their sorceries. The word "*sorcery*" in the Greek means *drugs*. In other words, this means they did not repent of their drug use and abuse.

In the midst of all the chaos taking place on the Earth, a marvelous thing occurring for the Nation and Children of Israel. In 70 A.D., the holy temple at Jerusalem was destroyed by the Romans. Many Israelites were killed and many more were taken away captive to all nations leaving them without their homeland, and without a holy temple to in which to worship (Luke 21:24). However, with the signing of the peace agreement, the holy temple will be rebuilt, only to be destroyed again by the Antichrist.

"¹And there was given me a reed like unto a rod: and the angel stood, saying, Rise, and measure the temple of God, and the altar, and them that worship therein. ²But the court which is without the temple leave out, and measure it not; for it is given unto the Gentiles: and the holy city shall they tread under foot forty and two months."

Revelation 11:1-2 (KJV)

In Revelation 11:3-12, two of Israel's greatest prophets, Moses and Elijah, or Enoch and Elijah, will be called upon to preach the gospel to the Israelites and to prophesy for 1,260 days. They will be a great threat to the Antichrist and many of those remaining on Earth will hate them. Once they have completed their assignment, they will both be killed and their dead bodies will be left to laying in the streets, for all to see, for 3½ days. After that period of time, the Spirit of God will resurrect them. They will stand on their feet and ascend up to Heaven, as they are caught up in a cloud.

As we transition into chapter 12 of the book of Revelation, we see there has been war in Heaven and there is a great conflict occurring on the Earth. Satan and his angels will be cast out of Heaven where they have been accusing the brethren before our God. In Revelation 13, things begin to dramatically shift as a beast is seen rising up out of the sea. The Antichrist will have power over the world government, which will consist of 10 kingdoms. The prophet, Daniel, made mention of this in Daniel 2:40-45.

Looking back at Revelation 13:11, we see that the Antichrist has assistance from someone. Many scholars believe it to be the false prophet; who has power to work wonders on the Earth. He is the beast referred to in this verse. Because of the miracles he will perform, many who remain on Earth will be deceived and, as a result, will worship the Antichrist and his image that has been created and erected.

The Antichrist and false prophet working together, along with the world governments, will take a massive toll on the world, on the Nation of Israel, and the Israelites themselves. This time is referred to as, "Jacob's trouble" (Jeremiah 30:7). Jesus also spoke of these events in Matthew 24:15-21:

"15When ye therefore shall see the abomination of desolation, spoken of by Daniel the prophet stand in the holy place, (whoso readeth, let him understand:) 16Then let them which be in Judaea flee into the mountains: 17Let him which is on the housetop not come down to take any thing out of his house: 18Neither let him which is in the field return back to take his clothes. 19And woe unto them that are with child, and to them that give suck in those days! 20But pray ye that your flight be not in the winter, neither on the sabbath day: 21For then shall be great tribulation, such as was not since the beginning of the world to this time, no, nor ever shall be."

What events trigger the abomination? The Antichrist will go into the newly built Temple at Jerusalem, as mentioned in Revelation 11, and will declare himself to be God, causing the daily sacrifices to cease. The children of Israel will know exactly who he is. From this moment on, the Antichrist and the false prophet mentioned in chapter 13, will have a great effect on the economy. They will cause many rich, poor, free and bond to receive a mark in their foreheads or on their hand. Without that mark, no man will be able to buy or sell.

"16And he causeth all, both small and great, rich and poor, free and bond to receive a mark in their right hand, or in their foreheads: 17And that no man might buy or sell, save he that had the mark, or the name of the beast, or the number of his name. 18Here is wisdom. Let him that hath understanding count the number of the beast: for it is the number of a man; and his number is Six hundred threescore and six."

Revelation 13:16-18 (KJV)

In Revelation 14, it is noted that the gospel will be preached by an angel, the 144,000 Israelites, and the two messengers (prophets) who were sent by God. There is much praise given to those who die during this time of great suffering as they did not receive the mark of the beast but suffered starvation, persecution, and torture, while confessing the name of Jesus.

Revelation 15 and16, gives us details of the last seven plagues which will be unleashed. They are known as the bowl judgments. These judgments come in quick succession as the seven vials are poured out by seven angels upon the Earth. It is best described as the, "full wrath of God". In the Greek, the word *"wrath"* means *passion, as if breathing hard, fierceness, indignation, wrath* (Strong's Concordance #2372). This meaning of the word wrath is not used until Revelation 12. What is the significance of this definition of the word? This *"wrath"* is that which God promised to deliver us from in 1 Thessalonians 5:9. It means *"desire as a reaching for excitement of the mind; violent passion or (ire, or [justifiable] abhorrence); by imply. punishment: anger, indignation, vengeance, wrath"* (Strong's Concordance #3709). Those holding to the mid-tribulation view, believing we will be raptured forty-two months into the 7-year tribulation, have an incorrect understanding of how the word "wrath" is being used.

As the first angel begins to pour out the first vial, sores will appear on those who bear the mark of the beast and those who worship his image. When the second angel pours its vial out upon the sea, it will become as the blood of a dead man and every living creature in the sea will die. With the pouring out of the third vial upon the rivers and fountains of water, they will become blood.

The fourth angel will pour its vial out upon the sun, and he will have the power to scorch men with fire. Those who are scorched will blaspheme the name of God. They will further refuse to repent and give glory to Him. The fifth angel will pour its vial out upon the seat of the beast. As a result, it throws the world dominion of the Antichrist into confusion. This judgment falls directly on the headquarters and their followers.

As the sixth angel pours its vial out, it causes the Euphrates rivers to dry up. This is to prepare the way for the "Kings of the East as they get ready for the greatest battle in history; the Battle of Armageddon. The "Kings of the East", are nations from the Orient who will be influenced by demonic spirit; that the purpose of the Almighty God will be fulfilled. These evil spirits will perform miracles, causing the rulers of nations to be demonized and deceived by Satan. The Battle of Armageddon will start near the end of the Tribulation Period, and conclude when Christ our Lord returns to destroy the wicked and deliver His people.

When the seventh angel pours out its vial, God will remember Great Babylon. As we move into Revelation 17, it is important to note that there are two Babylon's mentioned here. Although the meaning of Babylon in Revelation 17 and 18 is widely debated among scholars, most do agree that there is a religious Babylon and a political or commercial Babylon. Let's examine these scriptures more closely.

"¹And there came one of the seven angels which had the seven vials, and talked with me, saying unto me, Come hither; I will shew unto thee the judgment and the great whore that sitteth upon many water: ²With whom the kings of the earth have committed fornication, and the inhabitants of the earth have made drunk with the wine of her fornication. ³So he carried me away in the spirit into the wilderness: and I saw a woman sit upon a scarlet coloured beast, full of names of blasphemy, having seven heads and ten horns. ⁴And the woman was arrayed in purple and scarlet colour, and decked with gold and precious stones and pearls, having a golden cup in her hand full of abominations and filthiness of her fornication: ⁵And upon her forehead was a name written, MYSTERY, BABYLON THE GREAT, THE MOTHER OF HARLOTS AND ABOMINATIONS OF THE EARTH. ⁶And I saw the woman drunken with the blood of the saints,

and with the blood of the martyrs of Jesus: and when I saw her, I wondered with great admiration. 7And the angel said unto me, Wherefore didst thou marvel? I will tell thee the mystery of the woman, and of the beast that carrieth her, which hath the seven heads and ten horns. 8The beast that thou sawest was, and is not; and shall ascend out of the bottomless pit, and go into perdition: and they that dwell on the earth shall wonder, whose names were not written in the book of life from the foundation of the world, when they behold the beast that was, and is not, and yet is. 9And here is the mind which hath wisdom. The seven heads are seven mountains, on which the woman sitteth. 10And there are seven kings: five are fallen, and one is, and the other is not yet come; and when he cometh, he must continue a short space. 11And the beast that was, and is not, even he is the eighth, and if of the seven, and goeth into perdition. 12And the ten horns which thou sawest are ten kings, which have received no kingdom as yet; but receive power as kings on hour with the beast. 13These have one mind, and shall give their power and strength unto the beast. 14These shall make war with the Lamb, and the Lamb shall overcome them: for he is Lord of lords

and King of kings: and they that are with him are
called, and chosen, and faithful. ¹⁵*And he saith unto*
me, The waters which thou sawest, where the whore
sitteth, are peoples, and multitudes, and nations, and
tongues. ¹⁶*And the ten horns which thou sawest upon*
the beast, these shall hate the whore, and shall make
her desolate and naked, and shall eat her flesh, and
burn her with fire. ¹⁷*For God hath put in their hearts*
to fulfil his will, and to agree, and give their kingdom
unto the beast, until the words of God shall be
fulfilled. ¹⁸*And the woman which thou sawest is that*
great city, which reigneth over the kings of the
earth."

Revelation 17 (KJV)

This great whore, whom we just read so much about, represents religious Babylon, and encompasses all false religions. Please note, some of these false religions will include apostate Christianity, those who refuse to follow or obey the Word of God as it is given to us. Those Christians who were lukewarm, will not escape the wrath of God. We are commanded in 1 John 2:15, "to love not the world, neither the **things** that are in the world. If any man love the world, the love of the Father is not in him." As believers, we are not to be caught up with this world system and its operation independent of God.

It is my belief that one of the reasons these apostate Christians will be a part of the religious Babylon, is because of the lust of the flesh, the lust of the eye, and the pride of life. There are Christian leaders who teach once saved always saved. They deceive people with cheap grace, causing them to believe they don't have to change their lifestyles when they accept Christ as their personal Savior.

The Bible teaches, "If any man be in Christ, he is a new creature" (2 Corinthians 5:17). Jesus Christ warns us, that not all who profess salvation with their mouth, will make it into the kingdom; not all who say Lord, Lord will enter into the kingdom" (Matthew 7:21-23). Salvation has to be in the heart. This religious system will reject the teachings of the Apostles which proclaimed that there is no other way unto salvation, but by Jesus Christ and Him alone. Jesus told, His disciples, "I am the way, the truth, and the life: no man cometh unto the father, but by me" (John 14:6).

Those who hold to this view will suffer greatly, as God will judge religious Babylon during the Great Tribulation. The Antichrist and all his followers will turn, hate the whore, and ultimately, will utterly destroy religious Babylon.

God will put it in their hearts in order to fulfill His divine plan, and judgment will fall on her. The question many will now have is, why would the Antichrist turn against religious Babylon? An argument can be made that because the Antichrist goes into the newly built Temple at Jerusalem during the beginning of the great tribulation, which is the last forty-two months of the seven-year period, and declares himself to be God, he will no longer have any desire to share the spotlight or glory with religious Babylon. He is the father of lies and master deceiver. Satan has never kept his word!

Although some eschatology teachers believe, religious Babylon and political Babylon are the same, there is a problem with that argument. Religious Babylon is destroyed by the Antichrist and his supporters, while political Babylon will be destroyed by Jesus Christ. When political Babylon is destroyed, the people cry, as seen in the subsequent scriptures. Political Babylon is described in the Word of God as Babylon the Great.

"¹And after these things I saw another angel come down from heaven, having great power; and the earth was lightened with his glory. ²And he cried mightily with a strong voice, saying, Babylon the great is fallen, is fallen, and is become the habitation of devils, and the hold of every foul spirit, and a cage of every unclean and hateful bird. ³For all nations have drunk of the wine of the wrath of her fornication, and the kings of the earth have committed fornication with her, and the merchants of the earth are waxed rich through the abundance of her delicacies. ⁴And I heard another voice from heaven, saying, Come out of her, my people, that ye be not partakers of her sins, and that ye receive not of her plagues. ⁵For her sins have reached unto heaven, and God hath remembered her iniquities. ⁶Reward her even as she rewarded you, and double unto her double according to her works: in the cup which she hath filled fill to her double. ⁷How much she hath glorified herself, and lived deliciously, so much torment and sorrow give her: for she saith in her

heart, I sit a queen, and am no widow, and shall see no sorrow. ⁸Therefore shall her plagues come in one day, death, and mourning, and famine; and she shall be utterly burned with fire: for strong is the Lord God who judgeth her. ⁹And the kings of the earth, who have committed fornication and lived deliciously with her, shall bewail her, and lament for her, when they shall see the smoke of her burning, ¹⁰Standing afar off for the fear of her torment, saying, Alas, alas, that great city Babylon, that mighty city! For in one hour is they judgment come."

Revelation 18:1-10 (KJV)

As you continue reading you will see, there are 24 more complaints God makes against political Babylon. Examining these verses will help us determine exactly who Babylon the Great is. Scholars have presented a number of interpretations. Some scholars believe this Babylon is a literal state or country, while others believe it represents the whole ungodly world system brought under the Antichrist's rule. What is known for sure is that this Babylon operates strongly both commercially and politically, and her punishment and judgment is severe.

In my humble opinion, Babylon the Great, as mentioned in Revelation 18:1-24, is the United States of America (USA). This country is the only one that fits the description of her greatness. No other country has risen to the height, commercially and politically as we have, and in no other country has the Gospel been preached more than in the United States of America.

Commercial Babylon is very proud of all of her successes and dealings with other countries. The influence she possesses on all other nations is noted by God in verse 11. There is a plea for the people of God, to come out from following her before they are partakers of her sins. The judgment that befalls her will be so severe, that even those who have not received the mark of the beast, nor worshipped the Antichrist, and are keeping their faith in Christ Jesus the Lord, will not escape God's judgment if they are caught in Babylon at the appointed time of destruction.

Revelation 18:13, gives us another example as to why I believe political Babylon is the United States. The later part of this verse refers to merchandise being sold and traded in the country. It specifically mentions, humans being sold as slaves, as translated in the New

International Version (NIV) of the Bible. God has never forgotten how she treated those who were sold as slaves, during the Atlantic slave trade of 1619.

Several similarities between Babylon the Great, and the prophecies spoken by Isaiah the prophet are found in Isaiah 47:1-15.

"I was angry with my people and desecrated my inheritance; I gave them into your hand, and you showed them no mercy. Even on the aged you laid a very heavy yoke."

Isaiah 47:6 (NIV)

God allowed the children of Israel (Hebrew Israelites) to be carried away into slavery, because they did not keep the law as spoken of in Deuteronomy 28:16-68. The prophet Jeremiah also prophesied against Babylon (Jeremiah 51). Comparing these two prophecies, the two Babylon's have a several similarities as found in Revelation 18. With the destruction of Babylon the Great, the 7-year Tribulation Period will come to an end, and as the seventh angel pours its vial out on Babylon the Great, it will bring a close to the 21 judgments of God.

⌘ CHAPTER FOUR ⌘

The Second Coming of Jesus Christ

Jesus Christ makes reference to what will happen immediately after the tribulation in Matthew 24:29-31. It reads:

"29Immediately after the tribulation of those days shall the sun be darkened, and the moon shall not give her light, and the stars shall fall from heaven, and the powers of the heavens shall be shaken: 30And then shall appear the sign of the Son of man in heaven: and then shall all the tribes of earth mourn, and they shall see the Son of man coming in the clouds of heaven with power and great glory. 31And he shall send his angels with a great sound of a trumpet, and they shall gather together his elect from the four winds, from one end of heaven to the other."

It is important to note, that although we do not know the day nor the hour when the Lord shall return, we do know for certain that it will be immediately after the 70th week of Daniel, which is also known as the Tribulation Period. Each week represents a 7-year period. So, Jesus Christ will, without doubt, return in the future at the close of the 7-year Tribulation Period.

Because the Tribulation Period has not yet occurred, we know that it is a **future** event. There are those who hold to the view that Christ will never return because all things were fulfilled in the past with the destruction of the Jewish temple in A.D. 70. This is a gross misunderstanding of scripture.

When Jesus first came to the Earth, over 2000 years ago, many of the children of Israel rejected His teachings because they did not fully understand the holy scriptures nor the writings of the prophets. For example, the prophets who spoke of the coming of the Lord, spoke of both his first coming and second coming. Many read their writings, but did not have the ability to interpret them accurately. This resulted in great confusion, because some of the prophecies spoke of His second coming, while others spoke of His first coming.

This left some of the Israelites believing, there would only be one coming, and that coming would involve Jesus sitting on the throne of David, restoring the kingdom to Israel.

Let's reference some scriptures to see how some of the
Israelites became confused between the first and
second coming. Isaiah 11:1-10 reads:

*"1And there shall come forth a rod out of the stem of
Jesse, and a Branch shall grow out of his roots: 2And
the spirit of the Lord shall rest upon him, the spirit of
wisdom and understanding, the spirit of counsel and
might, the spirit of knowledge and of the fear of the
Lord; 3And shall make him of quick understanding in
the fear of the Lord: and he shall not judge after the
sight of his eyes, neither reprove after the hearing of
his ears: 4But with righteousness shall he judge the
poor, and reprove with equity for the meek of the
earth: and he shall smite the earth with the rod of his
mouth, and with the breath of his lips shall he slay
the wicked. 5And righteousness shall be the girdle of
his reins. 6The wolf also shall dwell with the lamb,
and the leopard shall die down with the kid; and the
calf and the young lion and the fatling together; and
a little child shall lead them. 7And the cow and the
bear shall feed; their young ones shall lie down
together: and the lion shall eat straw like the ox.
8And the sucking child shall play on the hole of the*

asp, and the weaned child shall put his hand on the cockatrice' den. ⁹They shall not hurt nor destroy in all my holy mountain: for the earth shall be full of the knowledge of the Lord, as the waters cover the sea. ¹⁰And in that day there shall be a root of Jesse, which shall stand for an ensign of the people; to it shall the Gentiles seek: and his rest shall be glorious."

In these verses, the prophet Isaiah was speaking of the coming of the Lord. Many of the Israelites were looking for the Messiah to come in fulfillment of these passages of scripture. However, they failed to realize that these scriptures speak of the Messiah's second coming. The Messiah will sit on the throne of David and rule over the whole Earth. Many of the children of Israel's eyes were blinded to the truths written by the prophet Isaiah.

In these verses, the prophet shows us that, upon His return, the Messiah would wreak havoc on the wicked who are on the Earth. He will punish all the wicked, then there will be a great time of peace, as it is revealed to us in the preceding passage of scripture.

It is easy to see how the Israelites of Jesus' time could have misinterpreted these scriptures and gotten confused, because when Jesus came, He was crucified. These scriptures mention nothing of that.

It is also important to point out the belief (by some) that the church has replaced the children of Israel; this again is extremely incorrect. Romans 11:1-10 reads:

"1I say then, Hath God cast away his people? God forbid. For I also am an Israelite, of the seed of Abraham, of the tribe of Benjamin. 2God hath not cast away his people which he foreknew. Wot ye not what the scripture saith of Elias? how he maketh intercession to God against Israel saying, 3Lord, they have killed thy prophets, and digged down thine altars; and I am left alone, and they seek my life. 4But what saith the answer of God unto him? I have reserved to myself seven thousand men, who have not bowed the knee to the image of Baal. 5Even so then at this present time also there is a remnant according to the election of grace. 6And if by grace, then is it no more of works: otherwise grace is no more grace. But if it be of works, then is it no more grace: otherwise work is no more work. 7What then? Israel hath not obtained that which he seeketh for; but the election hath obtained it, and the rest were blinded

8(According as it is written, God hath given them the spirit of slumber, eyes that they should not see, and ears that they should not hear;) unto this day. 9And David saith, Let their table be made a snare, and a trap, and a stumblingblock, and a recompence unto them: 10Let their eyes be darkened, that they may not see, and bow down their back alway. 11 I say then, Have they stumbled that they should fall? God forbid: but rather through their fall salvation is come unto the Gentiles, for to provoke them to jealousy. 12Now if the fall of them be the riches of the world, and the diminishing of them the riches of the Gentiles; how much more their fulness? 13For I speak to you Gentiles, inasmuch as I am the apostle of the Gentiles, I magnify mine office: 14If by any means I may provoke to emulation them which are my flesh, and might save some of them."

God has a covenant relationship with the Israelites. He may have gotten mad, and as a result, blinded their eyes intentionally and purposefully. You and I may or may not agree with His reasoning, but it is simply because of His divine purpose. We often question God's reasoning and the decisions He makes, especially when we have no control over them. His word declares He will have mercy and compassion on who He chooses (Romans 9:15). God is in control and working behind the scenes, causing things to happen according to His divine plan and purpose.

The erroneous belief that the Israelites are replaced with the church is answered in verse 11. The Israelites were not replaced by church, but God, in His infinite wisdom and graciousness, used the disobedience and fall of the Israelites to provide a means for the Gentiles to receive salvation as well.

Many, at that time, and even more so now, have yet to hear the Gospel. Jesus is allowing every nation and tongue to have the opportunity to accept Him as their personal savior and have the chance to receive eternal life in heaven. It was also to provoke the children of Israel to jealousy with the hope that their jealously would return them to their one true God.

A few verses later, in verse 26, we see that the Apostle Paul also reveals God's plan of restoration, stating, "there shall come out of Sion the Deliverer, and shall turn away ungodliness from Jacob." This is the same Jacob whose name was changed to Israel.

The apostles, who followed Christ, also had questions for Him. They too were a bit confused regarding what would happen to Him, and what His plans were for the future, as it was foretold by the prophets of old. Acts 1:6 says, "When they therefore were come together, they asked of him, saying, Lord, wilt thou at this time restore again the kingdom of Israel?" As it pertains to Christ coming to restore the kingdom of Israel, and sitting on the throne of David, they too, expected prophecy to be fulfilled with this coming.

The second coming of Jesus Christ was foretold by the prophets of old. They saw the day coming when the Messiah would reign on the Earth and sit on the throne of David, immediately after the Tribulation Period and upon His return.

The purpose of Christ returning back is to restore the Kingdom to Israel, and to gather all twelve tribes of Israel in their own homeland again; which is the state of Israel. The prophet, Ezekiel, saw the day of restoration coming to the whole House of Israel in Ezekiel 37:1-14.

He was told to prophesy to the dry bones, which are a symbol of the whole House of Israel. As a result of the prophecies spoken over those bones, Israel would receive a future restoration both physically and spiritually.

In order for Christ to sit on the throne of David, and reign as king in the Holy Land, He must reclaim the kingdoms of the world after the Tribulation Period. Christ had to come as the Lamb of God at His first coming. The first man that God created, Adam, opened the door to the dilemma of sin. The scriptures say, "the wages of sin is death, but the gift of God is eternal through Jesus Christ" (Romans 6:23).

Jesus, our Messiah payed the ransom over 2000 years ago, resolving the sin problem Adam got us into. It is so important for you and I to understand that our Messiah, in hanging on the cross and dying for all humanity, brought us back into right relationship with the Almighty God. It is important for you to put your faith and trust in Him so that you are not deceived. Jesus told Nicodemus, "except a man be born again, he cannot see the kingdom of God" (John 3:3). One must be born of water and of the Spirit (John 3:5).

With Jesus' second coming, He will not return as the Lamb of God, but as King of Kings. Christ said He would return immediately after the Great Tribulation. Revelation 19:11-16 gives us a picture of His return:

"11And I saw heaven opened, and behold a white horse; and he that sat upon him was called Faithful and True, and in righteousness he doth judge and make war. 12His eyes were as a flame of fire, and on his head were many crowns; and he had a name written, that no man knew, but he himself. 13And he was clothed with a vesture dipped in blood: and his name is called The Word of God. 14And the armies which were in heaven followed him upon white horses, clothed in fine linen, white and clean. 15And out of his mouth goeth a sharp sword, that with it he should smite the nations: and he shall rule them with a rod of iron: and he treadeth the winepress of the fierceness and wrath of Almighty God. 16And he hath on his vesture and on his thigh a name written, KING OF KINGS, AND LORD OF LORDS."

Most would think the world rulers would be glad to see the Messiah returning with His heavenly army, and the Bride of Christ, as revealed in Revelation 19:7-8.

However, Jesus returns prepared for a fearsome battle, as the kingdoms of the Earth, with the Antichrist and the false prophet leading, will not readily submit to His reign and authority.

The post-tribulation world will not freely surrender their kingdoms to the divine plan and purpose of the Almighty God. The Kingdom of God is righteousness, peace, and joy in the Holy Ghost (Romans 14:17). The kingdom of this world operates independent of God, as it wants to continue the lust of the eyes, the lust of the flesh, and the pride of life (1 John 2:16). The Kingdom of God, will be established in holiness, as God said, "Be ye holy, for I am holy" (1 Peter 1:16).

The second coming of Jesus Christ will be one to witness and it is my sincere belief that this will take place in our very near future. I encourage the Bride of Christ, the church, to make herself ready.

⌘ CHAPTER FIVE ⌘

The Battle of Armageddon

As Christ and His army return to the Earth, the Antichrist and the world governments will gather themselves together, in a place called Armageddon (Greek: harm-agedon). There has been much talk about this great battle. Many books have been written and messages preached surrounding it. So much so, that one would think the Bible would be riddled with the word. However, the word Armageddon only appears in the New Testament once and it speaks of a place that will host the greatest battle of all time.

Although I am not sure if it should be called that, as Christ and His army will win rather easily in spite of the fact that Satan, the Antichrist, will have assembled the greatest military force ever gathered in one place. All of the Asian nations, described as the Kings of the East, as well as all the nations of the world, who have aligned themselves with the Antichrist, will be gathered.

The preparation for this battle is described in Revelation 16:12-16. Again, examining these verses, we see that unclean spirits/demons will be unleashed by the dragon, who is a symbolic of Satan, and from the beast, and the false prophet. The purpose of the demonic spirits and activities manifesting, is to cause all the nations to be on one accord. These evil spirits will work miracles and, by the manifestation of their powers, it will become easy for the nations to be deceived into thinking that they will have a chance to win this great battle at Armageddon.

The prophet Joel saw the day coming for the restoration of his people, and that great battle with the world nations. Joel 3:1-4 reads:

"1For, behold, in those days, and in that time, when I shall bring again the captivity of Judah and Jerusalem, 2I will also gather all nations, and will bring them down into the valley of Jehoshaphat, and will plead with them there for my people and for my heritage Israel, whom they have scattered among the nations, and parted my land. 3And they have cast lots for my people; and have given a boy for a harlot, and sold a girl for wine, that they might drink. 4Yea, and what have ye to do with me, O Tyre, and Zidon, and all the coasts of Philistia? will ye render me a recompence? and if ye recompense me, swiftly and

speedily will I return your recompence upon your own head."

As we read these verses, it gives us a picture of the gathering of the nations to fight at this great battle. However, it also speaks of the Lord regathering the children of Judah, who were carried away as captives into all nations. Joel reveals the anger of God towards those nations which caused the Israelites to be scattered amongst the nations, after they parted His land. The Lord will not forget those nations who enslaved the Israelites and caused them great harm during those times of captivity.

The prophet Zephaniah also gives us great insight into this great battle in Zephaniah 3:8-20 saying:

"8Therefore wait ye upon me, saith the Lord, until the day that I rise up to the prey: for my determination is to gather the nations, that I may assemble the kingdoms, to pour upon them mine indignation, even all my fierce anger: for all the earth shall be devoured with the fire of my jealousy. 9For then will I turn to the people a pure language, that they may all call upon the name of the Lord, to serve him with one

consent. ¹⁰From beyond the rivers of Ethiopia my suppliants, even the daughter of my dispersed, shall bring mine offering. ¹¹In that day shalt thou not be ashamed for all they doings, wherein thou hast transgressed against me: for then I will take away out of the midst of thee them that rejoice in thy pride, and thou shalt no more be haughty because of my holy mountain. ¹²I will also leave in the midst of thee an afflicted and poor people, and they shall trust in the name of the Lord. ¹³The remnant of Israel shall not do iniquity, nor speak lies; neither shall a deceitful tongue be found in their mouth: for they shall feed and lie down, and none shall make them afraid. ¹⁴Sing, O daughter of Zion; shout, O Israel; be glad and rejoice with all the heart, O daughter of Jerusalem. ¹⁵The Lord hath taken away thy judgments, he hath cast out thine enemy: the kind of Israel, even the Lord, is in the midst of thee: thou shalt not see evil any more. ¹⁶In that day it shall be said to Jerusalem, Fear thou not: and to Zion, Let not thine hands be slack. ¹⁷The Lord thy God in the midst of thee is mighty; he will save, he will rejoice over thee with joy; he will rest in his love, he will joy over thee with singing. ¹⁸I will gather them that are sorrowful for the solemn assembly, who are of thee, to whom the reproach of it as a burden. ¹⁹Behold, at that time I will undo all that afflicted thee: and I will save her that halteth, and gather her that was driven out; and I will get them praise and fame in every land where they have been put to shame. ²⁰At that time will I bring you again, even in the time that I gather you: for I will make you a name and a praise among all people of the earth, when I turn back your captivity before your eyes, saith the Lord."

We are able to see through the prophetic eyes of these prophets what the future will look like, at the battle of Armageddon, and in the regathering of the Hebrew Israelites. I know you would like me to paint you a better picture of the great battle, but truthfully, this scene will be set in battle form, with the modern weapons that these countries will have. Millions of military soldiers that will be on display at Armageddon, or as some call it, the Valley of Jehoshaphat.

It will not be the "battle" that the Antichrist and his followers anticipated as Christ Jesus, who is King of kings and Lord of lords, will destroy all of their armies, with the words that come out of His mouth. This is described in Revelation 19:15: "And out of his mouth goeth a sharp sword, that with it he should smite the nations: and he shall rule them with a rod of iron: and he treadeth the winepress of the fierceness and wrath of Almighty God."

The devastation of this encounter will provide an abundance of food for the birds of the air and is recorded in Revelation 19:17-21:

"17And I saw and angel standing in the sun; and he cried with a loud voice, saying to all the fowls that fly in the midst of heaven, Come and gather yourselves together unto the supper of the great God; 18That ye may eat the flesh of kings, and the flesh of captains, and the flesh of mighty men, and the flesh of horses, and of them that sit on them, and the flesh of all men, both free and bond, both small and great. 19And I saw the beast, and the kings of the earth, and their armies, gathered together to make war against him that sat on the horse, and against his army. 20And the beast was taken, and with him the false prophet that wrought miracles before him, with which he deceived them that had received the mark of the beast, and them that worshipped his image. These

both were cast alive into a lake of fire burning with brimstone. ²¹And the remnant were slain with the sword of him that sat upon the horse, which sword proceeded out of his mouth: and all the fowls were filled with their flesh."

Although all the details of how the battle will be fought is not written in the Word of God, the victorious ending for Jesus and His followers is. We can be certain that what God has spoken regarding this battle will come to pass in the near future.

⌘ CHAPTER SIX ⌘

This Generation?

As we enter into this very important chapter, let's elaborate on the "generation" mentioned in Matthew 24:34. The scripture reads, "Verily I say unto you, This generation shall not pass, till all these things be fulfilled." In many cases, whenever the word "*generation*" appears in the New Testament, it speaks in reference to the people living at that particular time. The *Greek* word for "*generation*" is an "*age: the period or the person's, nation, time.*"

Numerous theories have been discussed concerning the end-time events and "this generation". Many have set dates, and those dates have come and gone. Some have tried to predict the generation referenced in Matthew 24:34, only to come up very short. The generation Christ refers to in this verse is not complicated, or difficult to figure out if one accurately breaks down the key verses spoken by Him.

Studying eschatology, is like a puzzle. When you look on the outside of the box, you get a complete picture of the puzzle. However, when you open the box, you have an abundance of small pieces that have to be put together **correctly** to form an accurate picture that matches the one on the outside of the box.

I know this has been said before, but I believe today's generation of people will be the ones to witness the return of Christ. I am confident that the body of people who are alive today is the generation foretold of by Christ; He cannot lie. What **has** happened, for the last two millennia, is that people have been either outright lying in pinpointing the truth, or just honestly mistaken. Along with everything else Jesus Christ spoke of in Matthew 24, He made reference to certain things that would take place preceding His return.

"4And Jesus answered and said unto them, Take heed that no man deceive you. 5For many shall come in my name, saying, I am Christ; and shall deceive many. 6And ye shall hear of wars and rumors of wars: see that ye be not troubled: for all these things must come to pass, but the end is not yet. 7For nation shall rise against nation, and kingdom against kingdom: and there shall be famines, and pestilences, and earthquakes, in divers places. 8All these are the beginning of sorrows. 9Then shall they deliver you up

to be afflicted, and shall kill you: and ye shall be
hated of all nations for my name's sake. ¹⁰And then
shall many be offended, and shall betray one another,
and shall hate one another. ¹¹And many false
prophets shall rise, and shall deceive many.

Matthew 24:4-11 (KJV)

The Word of God speaks of wars, of rumors of wars, and of people being deceived, but in verse 6, Jesus made it clear that the end was not yet. He gives us other important clues beginning in Matthew 24:7. There we are told, "nation shall rise against nation, and kingdom against kingdom." One who interprets this verse correctly will be able to determine who "this generation," spoken of in Matthew 24:34, is.

You may ask, why is that? Well, let's break down a few of these words starting with "*nation.*" Does "nation shall rise against nation" mean one country fighting against another country? For example, the United States vs. Russia, or China vs. Iraq? First, please note, the word "*nation*" is singular, not plural. The *Greek* word for *nation* is "*ethnos, a race as of the same habit, people.*" In other words, people living in the same nation will be rising up against one another. We have already seen this happening in this generation, amongst various countries including the United States. Another name for it is Civil War.

My prayer has always been, "Lord please don't let it happen in the United States." Scripture, however, will fulfill itself. We are beginning to see it happen right before our eyes; even in this great country called America.

One of Satan's tools of divisiveness for this country, and others, is race tensions. It is very challenging for a race of people to hold their peace, when they feel in their hearts that injustices are happening to them and to those they love. The enemy will magnify the killings of men and women of color, whether justified or unjustified, and use it as a means to bring us to war against one another. God will allow it, as it points to end times events and gets us closer to the events of the future.

Earthquakes and pestilence, such as Ebola outbreaks and coronavirus will occur, but Christ said, "these are only the beginning of sorrows" (Matthew 24:8). We know we are close to that time because we see these verses of scripture fulfilling themselves.

The key to understanding "this generation" is found, in Matthew 24:32. It reads:

"Now learn a parable of the fig tree; When his branch is yet tender, and putteth forth leaves, ye know that summer is nigh."

As a teacher of eschatology, I have seen this scripture misinterpreted by many, time and time again; including myself at one point in time. It is only after further research and guidance from the Spirit of Truth, that I believe I am now on the right track concerning its meaning.

In this passage of scripture, the fig tree represents the land of Israel, while the branches, represent the Israelites. Let's look at a couple of Old Testament scriptures that will help us expound on this. Hosea 9:10 says, "I found Israel like grapes in the wilderness; I saw your fathers as the firstripe in the fig tree at her first time: but they went to Baal-peor, and separated themselves unto that shame; and their abominations were according as they loved."

Here we see a fig tree used symbolically to represent Israel. Joel 1:7 says, "He hath laid my vine waste, and barked my fig tree: he hath made it clean bare, and cast it away; the branches thereof are made white." Once again, we see a fig tree is used to symbolize Israel. The Lord is saying that the fig tree or Israel will once again be recognized as a nation, in its land.

During the time Christ walked the earth, the Nation of Israel was under Roman control. After the destruction of the Temple at Jerusalem, the murdering of many Israelites, and scattering, and enslaving of many other Israelites, left the land bare. The land became populated with a different nationality of people, and the state of Israel was no longer recognized.

In 1948, the state of Israel was recognized again by the United Nations, and by other countries. Many were excited, believing that this was the fulfillment of Matthew 24:32. The problem with that was that the people who organized the events leading to the state being recognized again, were not descendants of the twelve tribes of Israel. Instead, they were converts or proselytes; people who converted to Judaism.

It was good that the converts were able to get the ball rolling, causing the state to be recognized again. However, the branches, the true Israelites, the blood descendants of Jacob, the twelve tribes of Israel, were still not present. One of the former presidents of Egypt stated they could not receive these new Jews, because they left out black, and returned white.

The ancient Israelites were warned by their God, in Deuteronomy 28:16-68, of the consequences of them not keeping the law. These consequences included being scattered amongst all the nations, becoming victim to various sicknesses and plagues, and even being sent into slavery where their wives would be raped by their slave masters. In addition, they would become borrowers instead of the lenders, and would suffer having their identity stripped away, with their history being erased.

However, the Lord promised to restore the natural branches of the fig tree. Sometime in the 1970s, a group of Africans were told by the Lord that they were descendants of Judah, and they were to return to Israel. Many of them, along with their leader, moved on the Word of the Lord. Many of them are still there to this day. In the 1980's and 1990's, the Israeli government airlifted Ethiopian Israelites, and brought them to their homeland. Those Ethiopian Israelites were found to be descendants of Levi and Judah. You may ask, how is that possible? Aren't Ethiopians the descendants of Ham, one of the sons of Noah, and Shem? Isn't he the line from which the Israelites descended? Yes, that is correct. However, we must remember the paternal lineage.

The Israelite lineage followed the males not the females. For instance, male Israelites could marry and father children with females whom descended from Ham, and their lineage would still remain. However, if a female Israelite married and mothered children from the descendants of Ham, Japheth, or anyone outside of the twelve tribes of Israel, their seed would no longer be considered as part of the Israelite bloodline.

In Acts 8:26-38, Philip, the evangelist, is found encountering an Ethiopian eunuch riding in a chariot and reading from the Torah. Be mindful that Gentiles were not walking around reading the holy writings of the prophets. This Ethiopian was a descendant of one of the twelve tribes of Israel. I feel the need to state this here, because many will argue that the branches are not black people. Although color is not a big issue with God, Truth is.

The fact of the matter is, the Israelites were and are a black-skinned people. As a baby, Moses was adopted by a daughter of Pharaoh and raised as Pharaoh's grandson (Exodus 2:6-10). Please note that ancient Egyptians (Mizraim) are listed in the table of nations in Genesis 10:6-20. What is my point? If the Egyptians are black (because all the descendants of Ham are black-skinned), how could Moses be mistaken, or able to pass as an Egyptian, if he was white.

Not convinced yet? In Exodus 2:18-21, Reuel was the father of seven daughters whom, upon their first encounter with Moses, received help with their flock. This resulted in their speedy return and prompted their father to question as to how they returned so quickly. The daughters responded saying, they had received help from an Egyptian. They too believed Moses was an Egyptian.

Marrying descendants of Ham was not uncommon for the Israelites. Looking at their genealogy, which Israelites are commanded to keep, will show it time and time again.

"18Now these are the generations of Pharez: Pharez begat Hezron, 19And Hezron begat Ram, and Ram begat Amminadab, 20And Amminadab begat Nahshon, and Nahshon begat Salmon, 21And Salmon begat Boaz, and Boaz begat Obed, and 22Obed begat Jesse, and Jesse begat David."

Ruth 4:18-22

Salmon married a Hamite woman named Rahab. She was a harlot in the land of Jericho. Boaz was their son and he married a Hamite woman named Ruth, a Moabite. Unto him, she bore a son named Jesse, and he bore David. This is the lineage from which Christ emerged. If that is not enough, Genesis 41:50-52 reads:

"50And unto Joseph were born two sons before the years of famine came, which Asenath the daughter of Potipherah priest of On bare unto him. 51And Joseph

called the name of firstborn Manasseh: For God, said he, hath made me forget all my toil, and all my father's house. [52] And the name of the second called he Ephraim: For God hath caused me to be fruitful in the land of my affliction".

Joseph is one of the descendants of the twelve tribes of Israel. He married a Hamite woman, and fathered two sons with her. The branches are not the Jews that we see in Israel today. As we observe the true branches, the true descendants of the twelve tribes of Israel, becoming aware of their identity and making others aware of it, we are witnessing the fulfillment of the beginning of Matthew 24:34.

I know some of you are shocked, and think I've totally missed the mark here, but consider what the scriptures say concerning the Jews living in the holy land today. Revelation 2:9 says, "I know thy works, and tribulation, and poverty, (but thou art rich) and I know the blasphemy of them which say they are Jews, and are not, but are the synagogue of Satan."

After the close of the first century A.D., the Ashkenazi people, those who converted to Judaism, began claiming to be Jews. In Revelation 3:8-9, God says the church of Philadelphia, which represents the church of our time, will be kept from the hour of temptation. It reads:

"8I know thy works: behold, I have set before thee an open door, and no man can shut it: for thou hast a little strength, and hast kept my word, and hast not denied my name. 9Behold, I will make them of the synagogue of Satan, which say they are Jews, and are not, but do lie; behold, I will make them to come and worship before thy feet, and to know that I have loved thee."

In these verses, we see that Christ was upset with those who pretended to be the natural branches (Israelites). It is important to note that the word *Jew* is only mentioned **twice** in the book of **Revelation**, and both times it is mentioned as a **rebuke**. Also take note that Ashkenazi Jews make up around 85% of Jews worldwide. Are you offended? Please understand it is not my intention to offend you. Let's go to the table of nations in Genesis 10:2-5, to see where these Jews descend from.

"2The sons of Japheth; Gomer, and Magog, and Madai, and Javan, and Tubal, and Meshech, and Tiras. 3And

the sons of Gomer; Ashkenaz, and Riphath, and Togarmah. ⁴And the sons of Javan; Elishah, and Tarshish, Kittim, and Dodanim. ⁵By these were the isles of the Gentiles divided into their lands; every one after his tongue, after their families, in their nations."

As we see here, Ashkenazi Jews are the descendants of Japheth, **not** Shem. The twelve tribes of Israel, those of the Israelites bloodline, are descendants of Shem.

So, what does all this mean? It means we need to look closely at the fig tree and the branches, especially as we move into the future, as the branches, the children of Israel (Hebrew Israelites) are becoming aware of who they truly are. It is in the plan of God to restore the identity of His people. Many will be surprised when they are made aware that the Hebrew Israelites' name was stripped from them while living in Spain and Portugal. It was at that time that they were then given the name Negro.

In an early edition of the Zondervan Compact Bible Dictionary, it was acknowledged that the Negroes were not descendants of Ham. The Lord is setting all things in order to precipitate the future return of Jesus Christ.

The sole purpose of the Israelites' identity being restored is to allow time for their eyes to be fully opened to their Messiah during the tribulation period. Many are unfamiliar with this level of teaching, especially in this context, but scripture cannot lie.

Previously, we discussed the sealing of the 144,000 Israelites in Revelation 7. They will be sent to accomplish a great evangelistic work, preaching the gospel mainly to the lost tribes of Israel who are scattered throughout the four corners of the world. I know you're wondering how is that possible, and why mainly the Hebrew Israelites?

We know the church is made up of Israelites and Gentiles. While the church remains on the Earth, the five-fold ministers, the apostles, prophets, evangelists, pastors, and teachers, are preaching the Gospel. During the rapture, once the church is removed from the Earth, God Almighty will turn His attention to His chosen people whose eyes were blinded. Read Romans 11:1-27, as it explains, the branches, the Hebrew Israelites, and the Gentiles being grafted in, in detail.

As I conclude this chapter, we see key pieces falling into place. Matthew 24:33 says, "So likewise ye, when ye shall see all these things, know that it is near, even at the doors." This verse identifies the generation who witnesses these things. As stated in verse 34, "Verily, I say to you, this generation shall not pass, till all these things be fulfilled." We are the generation witnessing those things now, and we are the generation who will witness the rapture of the church, the second coming of Jesus Christ, and the battle of Armageddon.

CHAPTER SEVEN

The Millennial Reign of Christ

The millennial reign of Christ refers to a 1,000-year period following the Battle of Armageddon, in which Christ will reign on the Earth along with His bride. Immediately after the Battle of Armageddon, Christ will sit on the throne of David in Jerusalem and begin to set things in order for His 1,000-year reign on Earth. One key thing that must be resolved is, Satan must be dealt with. Let's read Revelation 20:1-3:

"1And I saw and angel come down from heaven, having the key to the bottomless pit and a great chain in his hand. 2And he laid hold on the dragon, that old serpent, which is the Devil, and Satan, and bound him a thousand years, 3And cast him into the bottomless pit, and shut him up, and set a seal upon him, that he should deceive the nations no more, till the thousand years should be fulfilled: and after that he must be loosed a little season."

The prophet Isaiah also confirms this millennial reign in his book:

"⁶For unto us a child is born, unto us a son is given: and the government shall be upon his shoulder: and his name shall be called Wonderful, Counsellor, The mighty God, The everlasting Father, the Prince of Peace. ⁷Of the increase of his government and peace there shall be no end, upon the throne of David, and upon his kingdom, to order it, and to establish it with judgment and with justice from henceforth and even for ever. The zeal of the Lord of hosts will perform this."

Isaiah 9:6-7

The church, who became part of the army of the Lord during the during the Battle of Armageddon, and who returned back to Earth with Christ, will reign on the Earth with Him in our glorified bodies. Reference is made to this in Revelation 5:9-10:

"⁹And they sung a new song, saying, Thou art worthy to take the book, and to open the seals thereof: for thou wast slain, and hast redeemed us to God by thy blood out of every kindred, and tongue, and people, and nation; ¹⁰And hast made us unto our God kings and priest: and we shall reign on the earth."

What about all those who died during the tribulation? While their spirits are in Heaven, they do not yet have their glorified bodies because their physical bodies still rest in the grave, but Christ does not forget about them. They will be resurrected during the millennial reign. Revelation 20:4-6 says:

"4And I saw thrones, and they sat upon them, and judgment was given unto them: and I saw the souls of them that were beheaded for the witness of Jesus, and for the word of God, and which had not worshipped the beast, neither his image, neither had received his mark upon their foreheads, or in their hands; and they lived and reigned with Christ a thousand years. 5But the rest of the dead lived not again until the thousand years were finished. This is the first resurrection. 6Blessed and holy is he that hath part in the first resurrection: on such the second death hath no power but they shall be priests of God and of Christ, and shall reign with him a thousand years."

It is important to look closely at this passage of scripture as it reveals exactly who these people are. They are the ones who died during the Tribulation

Period. Notice it did not mention anything about the church being raptured at this time. Why? Because the rapture took place in Revelation 4. Notice these people were not called to meet the Lord in the air, as Paul said the church would be in 1 Thessalonians 4:16-17.

During this time, things are very peaceful. We are living in the presence of our Savior on Earth and all governments are following the commands given by Christ. People, with human bodies, will live in the presence of those with angelic bodies. For more details, let's see what the prophets Micah and Isaiah said concerning the millennial reign of Christ.

"¹But in the last days it shall come to pass, that the mountain of the house of the Lord shall be established in the top of the mountains, and it shall be exalted above the hills; and people shall flow unto it. ²And many nations shall come, and say, Come, and let us go up to the mountain of the Lord, and to the house of God of Jacob; and he will teach us of his ways, and we will walk in his paths: for the law shall go forth of Zion, and the word of the Lord from Jerusalem. ³And he shall judge among many people, and rebuke strong nations afar off; and they shall

beat their swords into plowshares, and their spears into pruninghooks: nation shall not lift up a sword against nation, neither shall they learn war any more. 4But they shall sit every man under his vine and under his fig tree; and none shall make them afraid: for the mouth of the Lord of hosts hath spoken it. 5For all people will walk every one in the name of his god, and we will walk in the name of the Lord our God for ever and ever. 6In that day, saith the Lord, will I assembles her that halteth, and I will gather her that is driven out, and her that I have afflicted; 7And I will make her that halted a remnant, and her that was cast afar off a strong nation: and the Lord shall reign over them in mount Zion from henceforth, even for ever. 8And thou, O tower of the flock, the strong hold of the daughter of Zion, unto thee shall it come, even the first dominion; the kingdom shall come to the daughter of Jerusalem."

Micah 4:1-8 (KJV)

"19And I will rejoice in Jerusalem, and joy in my people: and the voice of weeping shall be no more heard in her, nor the voice of crying. 20There shall be no more thence an infant of days, nor an old man that

hath not filled his days: for the child shall die an hundred years old; but the sinner being an hundred years old shall be accursed. ²¹And they shall build houses, and inhabit them; and they shall plant vineyards, and eat the fruit of them. ²²They shall not build, and another inhabit; they shall not plant, and another eat: for as the days of a tree are the days of my people, and mine elect shall long enjoy the work of their hands. ²³They shall not labour in vain, nor bring forth for trouble; for they are the seed of the blessed of the Lord, and their offspring with them. ²⁴And it shall come to pass, that before they call, I will answer; and while they are yet speaking, I will hear. ²⁵The wolf and the lamb shall feed together, and the lion shall eat straw like the bullock: and dust shall be the serpent's meat. They shall not hurt nor destroy in all my holy mountain, saith the Lord."

Isaiah 65:19-25

These two prophets enable us to have a clearer picture of the messianic Kingdom of Christ. The Word of God shares how life will be for those who did not die during the Tribulation Period, nor received the mark of the beast. Although people will still die, their lifespan will be much longer, compared to those living today.

There will no longer be a need to persevere in prayer during that time, for the Lord will dwell in the midst of us. Prayer will be answered without delay. Deadly, wild animals will be tamed at that time, and people will live in harmony and peace with one another.

As the 1,000-year reign comes to an end, it is important to note a few things that will transpire. First, Satan will be let loose out of his prison for a season.

"6Blessed and holy is he that hath part in the first resurrection: on such the second death has no power, but they shall be priests of God and of Christ, and shall reign with him a thousand years. 7And when the thousand years are expired, Satan shall be loosed out of his prison, 8And shall go out to deceive the nations which are in the four quarters of the earth, Gog and Magog, to gather them together to battle: the number of whom is as the sand of the sea. 8And they went up on the breadth of the earth, and compassed the camp of the saints about, and the beloved city: and the fire came down from God out of

heaven, and devoured them. ¹⁰And the devil that deceived them was cast into the lake of fire and brimstone, where the beast and the false prophet are, and shall be tormented day and night for ever and ever."

Revelation 20: 6-10 (KJV)

Satan's goal during this time will be to go out into the world and try to deceive as many people as he can. Some who are born during the 1,000-year reign of Christ will reject the holiness of God and the way of Christ. Many, having being convinced that they can overthrow God's kingdom, will choose to align with Satan. Ultimately, they will all be destroyed and thrown into the lake of fire along with Satan.

I believe God allows this last deception by Satan for those who are born during this time and for those who are unhappy with the reign of Christ and the lifestyle imposed upon them. Some will choose the wrong side and it will cost them an eternity, spent in the lake of fire.

⌘ CHAPTER EIGHT ⌘

The Great White Throne Judgment

This chapter will outline and answer questions many individuals have concerning what happens at death. While there are a lot of existing teachings on this topic, there are many who do not believe in the existence of Hell, or an eternal punishment for the wicked. We will examine this in more detail to determine if there is any truth to these concepts.

The Greek word for Hell is *"hades"* (Strong's Concordance #86). It is defined as, "the place of departed souls, grave, Hell." This is a place of torment for those who have not accepted Christ as their personal savior. Some hold the belief that this place is nonexistent, and that when one dies that's the end of it. This is not true. Jesus made reference to a place of torment for the wicked in Luke 16:19-31. It reads:

"19There was a certain rich man, which was clothed in purple and fine linen, and fared sumptuously every day: 20And there was a certain beggar named Lazarus, which was laid at his gate, full of sores, 21And desiring to be fed with the crumbs which fell

from the rich man's table: moreover the dogs came and licked his sores. 22And it came to pass, that the beggar died, and was carried by the angels into Abraham's bosom: the rich man also died, and was buried; 23And in hell he lift up his eyes, being in torments, and seeth Abraham afar off, and Lazarus in his bosom. 24And he cried and said, Father Abraham, have mercy on me, and send Lazarus, that he may dip the tip of his finger in water, and cool my tongue; for I am tormented in this flame. 25But Abraham said, Son, remember that thou in thy lifetime receivedst thy good things, and likewise Lazarus evil things: but now he is comforted, and thou art tormented. 26And beside all this, between us and you there is a great gulf fixed: so that they which would pass from hence to you cannot; neither can they pass to us, that would come from thence. 27Then he said, I pray thee therefore, that thou wouldest send him to my father's house. 28For I have five brethren; that he may testify unto them, lest they also come into this place of torment. 29Abraham saith unto him, They have Moses and the prophets; let them hear them. 30And he said, Nay, father Abraham: but if one went unto them from the dead, they will repent. 31And he said

unto him, If they hear not Moses and the prophets,
neither will they be persuaded, though one rose from
the dead."

As we see in the preceding scripture, this man is in a place of torment. There are is nothing we need to add to it. Instead of trusting God, he chose to trust his own wealth and live the lifestyle he wanted; as many do today. The great gulf, that is mentioned, was set in place before Christ was born. It separated Hell from what is called Abraham's bosom, a place of peace and rest.

Now that Christ has died and risen from the grave, that place of peace and rest is heaven. It is where Jesus went to prepare for His ascension. "To be absent from the body, is to be present with Christ" (2 Corinthians 5:8), but those who die without Christ, will go to this place of torment (Hades or Hell), until the Great White Throne Judgment.

Those who died apart from Christ, died during the millennial reign, or were Christians whose lives were not bearing fruit, as commanded by Christ, will find themselves in Hell first, then standing before God

Almighty at the Great White Throne Judgment. It is important to know that at the Great White Throne Judgment, you will get your day in court... sort of. For example, when one commits a crime, or is accused of a crime, the authorities take them to jail and locks them up until they go to court. After the court proceedings, if found guilty, they are sent to prison for whatever timeframe they were sentenced. God will administer judgment at the Great White Throne Judgment as mentioned in Revelation 20:11-15.

"11And I saw a great white throne, and him that sat on it, from whose face the earth and the heaven fled away; and there was found no place for them. 12And I saw the dead, small and great, stand before God; and the books were opened: and another book was opened, which is the book of life: and the dead were judged out of those things which were written in the books, according to their works. 13And the sea gave up the dead which were in it; and death and hell delivered up the dead which were in them: and they were judged every man according to their works. 14And the death and hell were cast into the lake of fire. This is the second death. 15And whosoever was

not found written in the book of life was cast into the lake of fire."

As we examine these verses, we see that people who find themselves standing before the Great White Throne are judged according to what was written in the books. They will see their whole lives before them. Every opportunity they've had to hear the Gospel, every idle word they spoke, and the sinful lives they lived will all be recorded in the books, and there will be no one to atone for their sins but Jesus Christ, whom they rejected.

Jesus Christ said, "I am the way, the truth, and the life; no one comes to the Father but by Me" (John 14:6). Jesus is the door to eternal life (John 10:9). "For God so loved the world, that He gave His only begotten Son that whosoever believeth in Him, shall have eternal life" (John 3:16).

Hell, a place of torment, is a holding place, while one awaits their court date at the Great White Throne Judgment. Notice, "death and hell were cast into the lake of fire" (Revelation 20:14). You may question, why would this happen? It is because death and hell are both temporary. From the time Adam and Eve sinned in the garden, God Almighty spoke of His Son as the solution for the sin problem. The Bible declares, that at the Great White Throne Judgment, whosoever's name is not written in the Book of Life, would be cast into the lake of fire.

If you should find yourself in Hell awaiting the Great White Throne Judgment, I regret to inform you, you will be found guilty and thrown into the lake of fire, which is the second death. Everyone who stands before the Great White Throne Judgment will have the opportunity to see their entire life shown to them, as everything you've ever done is recorded in books in Heaven.

There is good news though! The good news is, every evil and ungodly thing we have ever done can be erased by the blood of Jesus, if we make the choice and choose Him as our Savior. When we do, the blood of Jesus Christ, blots out our sins and washes us of all our iniquities. Those who have accepted Christ and are born again, will never stand before the Great White Throne Judgment. Instead, they will stand before the Judgment Seat of Christ, where rewards are issued to faithful believers. Unfortunately, there will be some who should receive rewards, but instead will suffer loss.

"13Every man's work shall be made manifest: for the day shall declare it, because it shall be revealed by fire; and the fire shall try every man's work of what sort it is. 14If any man's work abide which he hath built thereupon, he shall receive a reward. 15If any man's work shall be burned, he shall suffer loss: but he himself shall be saved; yet so as by fire."

1 Corinthians 3:13-15 (KJV)

As I conclude this chapter, I'd like to examine 1 Corinthians 3:13-14, and address another mistruth regarding what happens after death. There are some who teach that the second death means death without further torment. That is a misinterpretation of the truth. Revelation 20:10, teaches us about the lake of fire and its purpose for the duration of time. It reads:

"And the devil that deceived them was cast into the lake of fire and brimstone, where the beast and the false prophet are, and shall be tormented day and night for ever and ever."

One might believe this verse only pertains to the beast and the false prophet, but this is not true. The reason no one else is mentioned, is because the Great White Throne Judgment is spoken of after that. Remember Jesus Christ is the only person who can keep you and I from the Great White Throne Judgment and the eternal punishment of the lake of fire.

⌘ CHAPTER NINE ⌘

A New Heaven and Earth

As we look toward the future, the Lord reveals a time
after His return and subsequent defeat of the Antichrist,
and his followers, when He will create a new heaven
and a new earth. Isaiah 65:17 says, "For, behold, I
create new heavens and a new earth: and the former
shall not be remembered, nor come into mind." We can
look forward to a time when there will be no more
sorrow and no more pain or anguish.

The fall of man in the garden, resulted in a great deal of
suffering for all of humanity. When I speak of the
suffering, I am referring to the whole realm of things
that are endured by humans including sickness, pain,
misery, disappointments, poverty, mistreatment,
sorrow, persecution, and other kinds of trouble. We see
the floods, tornadoes, hurricanes, earthquakes, forest
fires, and all the other types of natural disasters, taking
place on Earth as a result of God's judgment. Creation
itself awaits a refreshing and a renewing by the
Almighty Creator, and God promises to make all things
new. Paul speaks of this in Romans 8:18-22. It says:

"18For I reckon that the sufferings of this present time are not worthy to be compared with the glory which shall be revealed in us. 19For the earnest expectation of the creature waiteth for the manifestation of the sons of God. 20For the creature was made subject to vanity, not willingly, but by reason of him who hat subjected the same in hope, 21Because the creature itself also shall be delivered from the bondage of corruption into the glorious liberty of the children of God. 22For we know that the whole creation groaneth and travaileth in pain together until now."

He will remove the memory of the former things, brought on by the fall of man in the garden, from our conscience. There is much debate by many scholars, as to how this will actually occur. Some hold to the belief that the world will be destroyed by fire. Others believe, when God speaks of creating a new heaven and a new earth, it will be more like a renovation. In any event, I look forward to the future and to the new Earth and new Heaven.

After the Great White Throne Judgment, we see where the Lord begins this undertaking.

"¹And I saw a new heaven and a new earth: for the first heaven and the first earth were passed away; and there was no more sea. ²And I John saw the holy city, new Jerusalem, coming down from God out of heaven, prepared as a bride adorned for her husband. ³And I heard a great voice out of heaven saying, Behold, the tabernacle of God is with men, and he will dwell with them, and they shall be his people, and God himself shall be with them, and be their God. ⁴And God shall wipe away all tears from their eyes; and there shall be no more death, neither sorrow, nor crying, neither shall there be any more pain: for the former things are passed away. ⁵And he that sat upon the throne said, Behold, I make all things new. And he said unto me, Write: for these words are true and faithful."

Revelation 21:1-5 (KJV)

The effect sin had on planet Earth as well as on humanity, is one of the main reasons for God making all things new. As we see signs of the end-times approaching, we must remain focused on Jesus Christ. It is becoming clearer that we are the generation who will see the return of Christ, and we do not want to miss what awaits us in the future, as it pertains to the new Heaven and the new Earth.

If that isn't enough to maintain our motivation to keep the faith, we need to know that there is also something very special awaiting the children of Israel and the Bride of Christ; it is called the New Jerusalem. When we consider the beauty and the splendor of this great city, as described in Revelation 21:10-27, the majesty and glory of it is almost incomprehensible to the human mind.

"10And he carried me away in the spirit to a great and high mountain, and shewed me that great city, the holy Jerusalem, descending out of heaven from God, 11Having the glory of God: and her light was like unto a stone most precious, even like a jasper stone, clear as crystal; 12And had a wall great and high, and had twelve gates, and at the gates twelve angels, and names written thereon, which are the names of the twelve tribes of the children of Israel: 13On the east three gates; on the north three gates; on the south three gates; and on the west three gates. 14And the wall of the city had twelve foundations, and in them the names of the twelve apostles of the Lamb. 15And

he that talked with me had a golden reed to measure the city, and the gates thereof, and the wall thereof. [16]*And the city lieth foursquare, and the length is as large as the breadth: and he measured the city with the reed, twelve thousand furlongs. The length and the breadth and the height of it are equal.* [17]*And he measured the wall thereof, an hundred and forty and four cubits, according to the measure of a man, that is, of the angel.* [18]*And the building of the wall of it was of jasper: and the city was pure gold, like unto clear glass.* [19]*And the foundations of the wall of the city were garnished with all manner of precious stones. The first foundation was jasper; the second sapphire; the third, a chalcedony; the fourth, an emerald;* [20]*The fifth sardonyx; the sixth, sardius; the seventh, chrysolite; the eighth, beryl; the ninth, a topaz; the tenth, a chrysoprasus; the eleventh, a jacinth; the twelfth, an amethyst.* [21]*And the twelve gates were twelve pearls; every several gate was of one pearl: and the street of the city was pure gold, as it were transparent glass."*

This great city, known as the Holy Jerusalem, will descend out of Heaven and rest above the new Heaven.

The Bible says there will be no need of the sun or moon to shine in it, for the glory of God would lighten it and the Lamb of God will be the light of it (Revelation 21:23). The nations living in the new city will have access to the New Jerusalem. Those living in the Holy Jerusalem are the Old Testament Israelites and the New Testament church. Notice that the twelve gates bear the names of the twelve tribes of Israel. When we look at the twelve foundations, they bear the names of the twelve apostles of the Lamb, who represent the church. It is important to note, when I make a distinction between the Israelites and the church, it is because the Bible does the same.

The Hebrew Israelites, also known as the Children of Israel, are God's covenant people. They are bloodline descendants of the twelve sons of Israel (Jacob) as well as those who became converts or proselytes in the Old Testament. The church is made up of Gentiles and Hebrew Israelites. Remember, Christ came for the lost sheep of the House of Israel (Matthew 15:2). As a result of them rejecting Him, salvation was given to the Gentiles, or as the Word of God says, "they were grafted in" (Romans 11:17).

God has intentionally blinded the eyes of the Hebrew Israelites, until the fullness of the Gentiles come in. Their rejection of the Messiah, opened the door for the Gentiles to come in. God's chosen people, the Israelites, endured severe pain and suffering while their eyes were blinded, but oh, how great the reward will be for those whose eyes are opened to the truth, who confess Jesus Christ as Lord and Messiah, who keep the faith, and endure to the end.

⌘ CHAPTER TEN ⌘

Wake Up Church

As we conclude, this chapter will focus on ensuring we are prepared to meet the Lord. As a young prophet, the word of the Lord came to me in 1993, saying we were the generation of Matthew 24:34, and that my assignment would be, to prepare a people for His coming. I am amazed to find that so many people are unprepared for the coming of the Lord. I believe the reason is because there is not enough sound teaching on it on the subject.

When Jesus Christ walked the Earth, He used the word *"watch,"* because He wanted the church to be ready to meet Him in the air. Before being crucified, He warned the church to *"watch"* because we would not know the hour of His return (Mark 13:33; Luke 21:36). The word *"watch"* means *to keep awake, watch, be vigilant, wake, be watchful* (Strong's Concordance #1127).

In Mark's Gospel, the word *"watch"* is used three times, as it pertained to Jesus' coming. Each time, Jesus is commanded His disciples to watch or keep awake. In other words, to continue to look for His coming. Jesus knew He would return to claim His church, and He did not want the bride to be unprepared. As a result, He gave clues regarding what to look for. We are currently seeing those signs unfold right before our eyes and many, in the church, assume that because they are saved, they don't need to be prepared. I totally disagree with that. Why? Because scripture speaks of staying awake. Mark 13:33-37 says:

"33 Take ye heed, watch and pray: for ye know not when the time is. 34For the Son of man is as a man taking a far journey, who left his house, and gave authority to his servants, and to every man his work, and commanded the porter to watch. 35Watch ye therefore: for ye know not when the master of the house cometh, at even, or at midnight, or at the cockcrowing, or in the morning: 36Lest coming suddenly he find you sleeping. 37And what I say unto you I say unto all, Watch."

I wonder if there will be consequence for believers who are caught sleeping, being unalert or unawake? I believe the point Christ is making is that we should be faithful to the Gospel of Jesus Christ and to the Word of God. We need to have love for Christ to the point that we keep His commandments and live our lives in a way that is pleasing to Him.

Many Christians believe they are living lifestyles that are pleasing to Him, but fail to understand that we must use the Word of God to measure our lifestyles. There are a few scriptures that we can use to help us measure whether or not our lives are lining up with the Word of God. Measuring our lives by the Word of God ensures we are being doers of the Word and not just hearers only (James 1:22).

Jesus stated, "But as the days of Noah were, so shall also the coming of the Son of man be" (Matthew 24:37). What was going on in Noah's day that led the Lord to make this statement? As we read through the scriptures, we see that it was business as usual. The people were eating, drinking, marrying, and being given into marriage, right up until the flood came and destroyed all but the eight souls aboard the ark. I believe Jesus references this story because it shows the element of surprise.

The people saw Noah building the ark, yet they made no attempt to change their lives. That warning is for believers. Just in case you think God will have mercy on you, think again. Babies, parents, grand-parents, aunts, etc., all died in the flood. Only eight people were spared. If God did not show mercy to the babies and the young then, He will not have mercy on us.

In Luke 13:24, Jesus said, "Strive to enter in at the strait gate: for many I say unto you, will seek to enter in, and shall not be able." The word "*strive*" means "*to struggle to compete for a prize, contend with an adversary, endeavored to accomplish something, fight, labor fervently*" (Strong's Concordance #75). The world has a different concept about life. Many of those concepts are rooted in the lust of the eyes, the lust of the flesh, and the pride of life, all of which are found outside of that narrow path.

Christ uses the phrase "weeping and gnashing of teeth" seven times in the New Testament. He knew people would think they were going to be with Him at the rapture and during His second return, but would be highly upset once they were rejected of Him.

My prayer is that this book will help you get prepared for that great day. Prayerfully, it has opened your eyes to the consequences of missing out.

In 2 Timothy 3:1-5, the Apostle Paul spoke the Word of the Lord concerning the last days. There, he paints a very disturbing image of the types of character people, who I believe is the church, would have.

"1 This know also, that in the last days perilous times shall come. 2 For shall be lovers of their own selves, covetous, boasters, proud, blasphemers, disobedient to parents, unthankful, unholy. Without natural affection, trucebreakers, false accusers, incontinent fierce, despisers of those that are good. 4 Traitors, heady, high-minded, lovers of the pleasures more than lovers of God. Having a form of godliness, but denying the power thereof: from such turn away."

Some argue that He is referring to the state of the world, but I believe there are certain words used which point to the individuals who make up the church. First of all, the world does not have a form of godliness, as they do not profess Christ, and they have no power in Christ to deny, so he is not speaking about the world, but about the state of the church and its decline. I can easily see how people will be weeping and gnashing their teeth. Many will have committed their lives to church attendance, with some even working in some type of auxiliary within the church, but their time will be expended only to be denied access into His eternal abode.

We must strive to realize and maintain the holiness and righteousness of God, and we must endeavor to always be ready for His return. Jesus warns the churches that He will "remove their candlestick," which represents a congregation under the church heading, from their destiny if they did not repent of their sins (Revelation 2-3). It's not enough just to confess you are saved. Our lives must be filled with the fruit of the Spirit. We must practice crucifying the flesh daily, knowing that, the rewards are great. Although it won't be easy, we must strive for the prize of eternal life with Christ Jesus.

We must also understand that there will be severe consequences if He says, "depart from Me." Jesus has sent many messengers, and released signs, and wonders into the world giving us clue after clue that His return is imminent. Those who are not prepared, will be left, and those who chose to be filthy, will be allowed to remain filthy. Revelation 22:10-20 reinforces this. It reads:

"10And he saith unto me, Seal not the sayings of prophecy of this book: for the time is at hand. 11He that is unjust, let him be unjust still: and he which is filthy, let him be filthy still: and he that is righteous, let him be righteous still: and he that is holy, let him be holy still. 12And, behold, I come quickly; and my reward is with me, to give every man according as his work shall be. 13I am Alpha and Omega, the beginning and the end, the first and the last. 14Blessed are they that do his commandments, that they may have right to the tree of life, and may enter in through the gates into the city. 15For without are dogs, and sorcerers, and whoremongers, and murders, and idolaters, and whosoever loveth and maketh a lie. 16I Jesus have sent mine angel to testify unto you these things in the churches. I am the root and the offspring of David, and the bright and morning star. 17And the Spirit and the bride say, Come. And let him that heareth say, Come. And let him that is athirst come. And whosoever will, let him take the water of life freely. 18For I testify unto every

man that heareth the words of the prophecy of this book, If any man shall add unto these things, God shall add unto him the plagues that are written in this book: ¹⁹And if any man shall take away from the words of the book of this prophecy, God shall take away his part out of the book of life, and out of the holy city, and from the things which are written in this book. ²⁰He which testifieth these things saith, Surely I come quickly. Amen. Even so, come, Lord Jesus."

I ask that everyone reading this book, to please be mindful of these things; keep them at the forefront of your heart and mind. First, many have loved ones who are gay, lesbian, transsexual, etc. They need to be prepared to meet the Lord. We cannot be afraid to talk to our loved ones about the truth. We can't be afraid to tell them about Jesus' love and the salvation He extends to everyone. The Lord will not have mercy on them if they don't repent before meeting Him. Love and treat them with respect, but continue to declare the truth to them; remember Sodom and Gomorrah.

Finally, to those who are struggling with unforgiveness and bitterness, we cannot obtain forgiveness of our sins, if we do not forgive the sins of others (Mark 11:26). Although we will struggle with the flesh, we have to crucify it daily. Holding on to offense only aides in weighing us down and, if we are not careful, will ultimately cause us to be denied access into Heaven. I urge you to secure your eternity in Heaven today by accepting Jesus Christ as your personal savior, lining your life up with the Word of God, and endeavoring to live in a way that pleases Him.

www.ingramcontent.com/pod-product-compliance
Lightning Source LLC
Chambersburg PA
CBHW052342090426
42740CB00028B/2800